LESSONS
FROM LANDON

Roberta,

May our stories
encourage you on
your journey.

Steven Blomberg

LESSONS FROM LANDON

THROUGH THE SEASONS OF LIFE

Steven Blomberg
Illustrations by Landon Blomberg

MeadowView Publishing
Ogema, WI

Scripture quotations are from *The Holy Bible, New International Version*, NIV.
Copyright 1973, 1978, 1984 by International Bible Society.

MeadowView Publishing
W2665 Hultman Lake Road
Ogema, WI 54459

Published in the United States of America
ISBN: 9781095315019

Dedication:

To my son **Landon**...you inspire me daily to be a better person.

To my wife **Krista**...you have kept me grounded on this journey. I could not have asked God for a more perfect partner in this venture we call life.

To my children **Joel**, **Michaela**, and **Olivia**...you all have brought me so much joy in parenting. You have given me affirmation while I worked at the job of parenting your brother, a young man with special needs. Your encouragement, understanding, and compassion for your brother have been more of an inspiration than you will ever know!

To my **Aunt Donna**...your help in editing, your encouragement in this endeavor, and your constant love and prayers for my family have all been priceless.

To my friend and mentor **Ginny**...thank you for your help in my final editing, for your brainstorm to have Landon illustrate his book, and for your own lessons which helped make me the teacher I became.

To **Amanda Jayne**...thank you for guiding Landon in illustrating his book.

Contents:

Preface:

Life is a journey...an amazing and unique journey filled with lessons and learning. Sometimes the learning is unexpected, and often the one we learn these lessons from is an even greater surprise.

I have been an educator for 33 years. In that time, I have prepared thousands of lessons. Preparation is part of a teacher's life. Hours of planning go into a successful unit of lessons. I have always relied heavily on organization and creativity to reach my students. I have thoroughly enjoyed my career as an educator.

As a parent, the lessons have been more spontaneous. Preparing for the unknown is not an easy task, even with a strong faith in God and my wonderful wife Krista by my side. Through the years of raising our four children there have been many uncharted waters to navigate, often leading us into places we never anticipated. Consequently, the lessons taught in our home often came in the moment, and sometimes not from us, but from our children.

This book is just that...lessons I have learned along the way while journeying with my son, Landon. Some I have learned as a result of life experiences we shared. Others I have learned by observing his resiliency to the difficulties in life. Until the summer of his fifth year I had no idea what was just ahead. The journey we would embark upon, as a family, would change us. We have had more than our share of rough roads along the way. Now, nineteen years later, I look back and see that those roads, those lessons have not only shaped Landon, but also us, his family, into individuals with more depth and strength of character.

Landon had his first tonic-clonic (grand mal) seizure on the first day of summer vacation when he was four years old. Were this a book on epilepsy, I would include lots of terms like "cortical dysplasia" and "postictal." Were this a book on epilepsy treatments, I would spend pages describing our tireless efforts to control Landon's seizures with diets, medications, naturopathy, CBD oil, and even brain mapping surgery. But this is a book of lessons I have learned from my son, who still struggles daily with seizures. They have affected his life greatly. If the seizures don't stop, he will never drive a car, he will probably never balance his own checkbook, and the likelihood of dating and marriage will be greatly diminished. His 23-year old body is a mixture of man and boy. He loves picture books, he loves snuggling with his parents during a movie, and he loves to color. He also loves to use tools, he loves to drive his four-wheeler, and he loves to dream of becoming a carpenter and going to college.

Landon has a disability. If I do my math correctly, he has had well over 20,000 seizures in his lifetime. The effect of those seizures has meant some degree of injury to his brain. However, Landon chooses not to focus on his disability. Instead he looks at his abilities, and he faces the challenges in his life with bravery.

What you hold in your hands is a book of hope...a book of life lessons...a book of living life to the fullest. Life is a series of seasons and journeys, sometimes over mountaintops and sometimes through deep valleys. During those times we are accompanied by others who bring meaning in the process. May the stories on these pages help you find encouragement in the journey of life you are traveling. May the tales recounted on these pages cause you to pause and ponder the road on which you traverse. May they challenge you to persevere and even find contentment amidst the battles you are facing. May they cause you to embrace life, itself, through the highs and the lows. May the stories of my son leave you changed.

In the Book of Ecclesiastes King Solomon stated that there is a time for everything. There is a time to be born and a time to die, but there is so much more between those two times. The moments, the emotions, the memories, and the lives that interact with our own are what bring life its richness, its flavor. In those moments, often without realizing it, we just may learn something that guides us to a place of wisdom, a place of acceptance, and a place of contentment. Those places may ultimately enrich our lives far more than we could ever have imagined.

A Time for Everything: Ecclesiastes 3:3-8

"There is a time for everything, and a season for every activity under the heavens:

a time to be born and a time to die,
a time to plant and a time to uproot,
a time to kill and a time to heal,
a time to tear down and a time to build,
a time to weep and a time to laugh,
a time to mourn and a time to dance,
a time to scatter stones and a time to gather them,
a time to embrace and a time to refrain from embracing,
a time to search and a time to give up,
a time to keep and a time to throw away,
a time to tear and a time to mend,
a time to be silent and a time to speak,
a time to love and a time to hate,
a time for war and a time for peace."

Introduction:

In many ways parenting is like other jobs in this world. It has great challenges and can have even greater rewards. My wife, Krista, and I have experienced both. As I prepared to write this book, I reflected on the stories to tell and the lessons to include in its pages. I wanted to focus on the positive traits of my son's character without giving the reader an unrealistic image of him. Please understand, he truly is a hero in my eyes, and he has an amazingly good heart. As you read these chapters from our lives, you will see his heart in action and the goodness he exudes in his life. However, aside from his disability and the struggles that accompany living with it, he also was, and still is, a normal child. He disobeyed, he challenged authority, and he fought with his siblings over toys and chores. So, in the telling of these stories I do not desire to put Landon on a pedestal. Rather, I have chosen to reflect on those moments when his good heart and his trusting spirit taught me lessons for my journey and allowed us to learn together.

CHAPTER 1:
Landon Arrives

L.B

By nature, I don't always see the good in people or in situations for that matter. I want to, but I don't. At times I can be downright pessimistic. In fact, at THAT moment I had an irritable attitude. It was a sweltering day. It wasn't just hot, but it was sticky, humid, and miserable. It was the kind of day that promises relief only when the clouds open and pelt the ground with much-too-large raindrops. It was August and the dog days of summer were upon us. My wife and I were building our first home and living with my parents at the time, which only added stress to the discomfort of the day.

Our 19-month-old son, Joel, had broken his femur a few weeks before and was in a body cast from his belly down to his ankle. This made diapering him and getting him into his car seat a challenge, to say the least. We had prepared him as well as we could for the near arrival of his brother. We were spending this muggy day picnicking with friends after church and trying to keep cool. Knowing that the summer was drawing to a close, and I would soon be back at school, we enjoyed our time together eating, playing yard games, and talking about how it would be a good day to have a baby.

Krista and I had Joel in his crib by 8:00 that evening, and since she was feeling achy and uncomfortable, she took a long bath. By 9:00 p.m. we were in bed thinking we should get some sleep since this might be the night. But sleep was evasive, as we had much on our minds. Plans for the new house were a common topic for discussion. We shared bits of our day, talked about Joel's love for Chance, the dog on my parents' farm, and finally drifted into a restless sleep.

At 10:30 p.m. Krista woke me to say it was time. "Are you sure?" I asked, and she assured me that she was. Her bag was packed and ready, so after waking my mom to tell her, we began the 60-mile drive to the hospital.

Though it was nighttime, the air was still stifling outside. As we left the driveway and turned onto the main road the rain started. Gentle at first, it soon developed into a torrent that matched the steady rhythm of the windshield wipers.

The contractions were now becoming more evident, but still manageable. Neither of us were worried. We had plenty of time. I was quiet as I concentrated on the road ahead. Krista tried to relax through the discomfort she was obviously feeling, now with more regularity.

Halfway to the hospital the floodgates of the sky opened. Driving suddenly became almost impossible. Krista was really starting to feel the contractions, and with the visibility down to a few feet, I began wondering about the distinct possibility that this baby could be born in a car! I had heard about cases like this. I knew of an aunt of mine who had been on her way to deliver her eighth child. Knowing they couldn't make it to the hospital, her husband had stopped at a small clinic on the way. While he was inside describing their plight, their child was born in the car. "What would I do...?" I silently asked myself.

Landon...Landon Kyle...we had chosen the name months before. I had come up with it and my wife had fallen in love with it. We had been talking to him for weeks, and even now asked him to wait just a little longer for our face-to-face meeting.

The lights of an oncoming car brought my focus back to our present dilemma. Due to the heavy rain, and with another twenty miles ahead of us, our current speed would dictate close to another hour on the road. I silently prayed that the rain would let up. I assured my wife that it would as I pushed the accelerator a bit more.

We had called ahead to the emergency room. I knew they would be ready for us since it was already past 11:30, the expected arrival time I had given them before the storm began. Krista's pregnancy, being high-risk, also assured us of quick attention once we were there. Another strong contraction...another bright flash of lightning. The storm seemed to be in synch with the labor pains needed to bring our son into the world. But the pelting rain and the car were out of rhythm.

This was so different than our first pregnancy. Joel, our oldest, had been born in January during a cold spell that lasted a week in Northern Wisconsin. Though not unheard of, the sixty below temperatures, during his delivery, had caught us off guard.

At last the intensity of the rain decreased, the visibility increased, and with it the speed of the car. I suddenly felt a bit more confidence that I would not have to deliver this baby alone. I pulled up to the entrance of the emergency room at 12:02 a.m. They were ready with a wheelchair.

As they wheeled Krista away, I parked the car. Within ten minutes we were in a birthing room. Krista was getting hooked up to monitors, and I was calling her parents to let them know this was it. Our visions of a relaxed labor with walks around the corridor of the hospital and games of cribbage vanished as I got off the phone. Krista, having had toxemia with her first pregnancy, was already hooked up to more wires than I could count. They were doing their job, showing vitals not only on her, but on our new son. Her labor continued for the next few hours, a bit slower than we expected. After an epidural, the pain decreased enough to allow Krista to rest between contractions.

At 3:45 Dr. Meyer was called in and the pushing ensued. At 4:06 in the morning, on August 7th, 1995, our son Landon Kyle was born. He weighed 8 pounds, 2 ½ ounces and was 21 inches long. His Apgar score was 9/9. As a father this didn't mean much to me. I was busy counting fingers and toes, cutting the cord, and thanking God for this precious gift.

August rains often bring relief from heat and humidity in Wisconsin. On this particular stormy night, they were accompanied by something much greater...new life! And just like that fierce storm brought with it something good...relief from the sweltering heat; those labor pains brought my new son into the world.

Storms impact us. They have the ability to change our situation and even change us in a moment. Storms and people are similar in this way. At that moment, I had no idea the profound influence that my new son would have on my life. Of course, I expected my son to affect me. I anticipated that with each new member of our family. However, I didn't picture this tiny babe, that I now held in my arms, teaching me and inspiring me in all the ways I can now see as I reflect on the years that we have shared.

So began my journey with Landon. Over the next 23 years he would positively demonstrate time and again how to look for the good in this world. A time to be born...a child entered the world and became a part of my life. This child would help me look for the good and also find it, even in the darkest of times we would travel together.

- Look for the positive things in this world.

CHAPTER 2:
Landon's Friend, Lynnette

L.B.

Friendships can be peculiar. We never know who will
enter our lives and make a lifelong investment, even in a
short amount of time. I have been blessed with a lot of
friends in this life. Some are so much like me that it's
almost comical. Others are complete opposites, but they
complement my strengths and weaknesses. I can't
imagine life without friends. Friendship, true friendship
takes time, commitment, and a degree of selflessness.

Most of Landon's friends during his growing up years
were his age. They wrestled, played at recess, had
water fights in the summer, went for hikes, and built forts
in the woods. His older brother, Joel, was one of his best
friends. Bike riding through mud puddles in the spring,
catching frogs and turtles in the summer, jumping in
raked leaves in the fall, and sledding down the driveway
hill in the winter were daily adventures for the two of
them. They made the most of these times! Weekly
hikes, if not daily, to Grandma's farm next door were a
favorite pastime any time of the year.

As Landon's seizures increased over his adolescent
years, so did his needed recovery time. He was lethargic
and tired most days. Keeping up with his peers became
more and more difficult, and although some very special
friends still spent time with him, the activities were much
more sedate. Without the physical ability to invest in his
friendships, we saw his circle of friends diminishing. His
peers at school were kind to him, but there was a fear of
how to deal with the realities of his seizures. Invitations
to birthday parties came less and less throughout his
elementary years. By middle school it was difficult for
Landon to even converse with others due to the
exhaustion he experienced. He would invite a friend over
and they would watch a movie together, but he often
spent most of the time sleeping. This tugged
at my father's heart and I hurt for my son, knowing how
valuable my friendships were to me.

Landon found his own way of dealing with this dilemma. He began to seek out friends who were older than him...much older...people who didn't demand activity or spontaneity. We would often find him at picnics or after church visiting with older men...his friends, as he called them. And they were his friends...dear people who invested in his life and affirmed him.

When Landon was nine years old, his seizures worsened despite the arsenal of medications taken daily. Each night he struggled with upwards of thirty grand mal seizures. This went on for eighteen months of his life. It was during this period he could no longer attend school regularly. Investing in childhood friendships was out of the question. Life was all about survival, getting food and meds into his little body, and daily recovering from the attack of seizures the night before. It was during this time that Lynnette entered Landon's life.

Lynnette was a woman who attended our church. She was 50 years Landon's senior and she taught math in a neighboring town. She was not an obvious choice of a friend for a young boy. In fact, Landon's only previous encounter with her was one Sunday morning when she had a display of coins and artifacts from a recent mission trip that she had taken. Temptation had gotten the best of him, and he had taken one of those shiny silver coins in the display. When we discovered it, Landon returned it with an apology and a promise to never steal again. As a parent, it is very humbling to have to admit to someone you have known all your life that your child stole from them...at church! Being a young father, it certainly made me feel like I had failed.

A few months passed after this interaction. One Sunday morning we learned that Lynnette had been diagnosed with cancer. As a family we prayed for her and for her healing. Landon especially took an interest in this woman who had forgiven him for stealing. As a family, we were exceptionally fragile during this eighteen-month period of cluster seizures. As parents we were worn, and we began to see how our other three children were being affected. We were exhausted yet attempting to focus on something other than the ever-present onslaught of seizures. We were greatly in need of a new perspective.

Most of Landon's seizures happened while he slept. The daytime ones were especially traumatizing for his siblings to witness. In an effort to help our family change our focus, Krista and I decided that each time Landon had a seizure during the day we would stop and pray for Lynnette. We needed to avert our focus from the enemy that was rocking our lives. This started a routine that would last for almost two years.

Over that time, Lynnette's cancer slowly spread, and although there were times of remission, it eventually became evident that she would lose the battle. Throughout her fight she regularly sent notes and cards to Landon in the mail, always including a dollar for him to spend on something. She faithfully prayed for Landon, as he did for her. During one especially bad week when Landon had already had over 100 grand mal seizures, he had yet another while going down the stairs to his room. He stumbled, fell down the stairs, and bit his tongue, a common occurrence during his seizures.

We waited for the minutes to tick off the clock and for the cessation of the seizure. Krista and I were both emotionally raw at the time. She was crying from her own exhaustion, and I was just angry with the world. As the seizure subsided, Landon gasped for breath and uttered, "We have to pray for Lynnette." I could hardly believe my ears. In his own pain and turmoil, he was focused on someone else.

This had been our plan and we had consistently done this, but in that moment during a horrific week we had shifted our focus back to OUR suffering. Landon, however, had not. As the tears flowed from our eyes, we prayed with him for our friend, Lynnette.

The following summer we were vacationing in South Dakota. We had weathered the year and a half of intense cluster seizures, and Landon's health was better than it had been for the past several years. Never knowing when things might suddenly turn bad again, we had decided it was a valuable time for a big family vacation. While there, we received word that Lynnette had lost her battle with cancer. We had somewhat expected it. As a family we decided to cut our vacation short and head home so that we could attend the funeral.

At the request of her family, Landon was a pallbearer at the funeral. My heart was grieved for the family of this dear woman. She had touched Landon's life, and she had touched ours in ways I don't believe she ever knew. She taught Landon lessons in friendship through her cards, encouragement, and short visits after church. She taught him about dying through her steadfast faith, which was evident at her funeral.

Due to his friendship with Lynnette, who struggled with her own battle alongside his, Landon learned the art of selflessness. He demonstrated it on that day on the stairs, and he left us with a vivid, mental image of what it looks like. It is a picture that will stay with me for the rest of my life.

Landon has rarely acted out with self-pity or resentment regarding his disability. He thinks of others and loves people for who they are, not for what he can get from them. Through his friendship with Lynnette he learned and demonstrated the art of putting others first, and he continues to display it often in his dealings with other friends.

When I reflect on the trait of selflessness I will always think of my son and that horrible, wonderful day. It was a time when a helpless, young boy thought of someone else and placed her needs above his own. Selflessness is an essential component in a true friendship. I see it in my son every day!

- Do something selfless for someone else, expecting nothing in return.

CHAPTER 3:
Gardening

I find gardening enjoyable. It takes time and effort, but it yields great rewards. Ever since I was a young child, I have gardened. I learned how to plant while working beside my mom in her large vegetable patch. At the time, it felt like her garden covered at least an acre of land. I believe we grew every vegetable known to modern man. We tilled and planted to provide food for the nine members of our family. I learned to love gardening. There is an innocent simplicity in the process. You drop an insignificant little seed into some dirt and with proper sunlight, water, and attention it grows into something valuable and satisfying.

My mom also had beautiful flower beds in her yard. She knew exactly what combinations of flowers would complement each other. Many of the flowers in my own yard came from her beautiful perennial gardens. Like most good things, gardens take time. Planting is just one stage of the process. Successful gardeners know that one must also watch, provide care, feed, and nurture...all at the right times.

I like a neat and orderly garden. I also like symmetry in its rows. Having young children help in a garden poses a problem to a slightly obsessed gardener, like myself. It took many summers and harvests before I learned the true lesson of gardening. At an early age, my children wanted to help plant. I wanted their help. I wanted them to learn to love the experience.

Occasionally tender tomato transplants were stepped upon or onion sets popped out of the ground due to little fingers and toes. And even though my mother always said, "You can't overwater a transplant," I found that with my children's help, she was wrong. Because of this, planting with my children became a bit of an anxious endeavor. I found it much easier to do it myself, however that defeated the purpose. I wanted them to learn the real lesson of planting a garden. It is to enjoy the process, the process of watching things grow as you patiently nurture them at just the right time

The benefits of planting and gardening are amazing! My children have learned the great satisfaction of harvesting and later enjoying the flavor of home-grown vegetables. Our freezers and our canning room provide tangible reminders of our hard work in the garden.

My vegetable garden is not nearly as large as my mother's garden was. We grow our favorite vegetables, but at a much smaller scale. My neighborhood is full of gardens, and neighbors are always willing to trade or give away extra produce. I look with admiration when I see tasty vegetables and beautiful flowers growing in these places.

I think all of us are gardeners. We are each planting and growing another type of garden in this life. It's the garden in which we spend time every day. It is the garden where we live and work. Some days we are called to plant and others we water. Unfortunately, sometimes we neglect the precious seedlings entrusted to us in this life garden. Other times we fail to harvest at the right time.

Landon has planted a lot of things throughout his life. His sparkling eyes have planted tender shoots of kindness into the lives of numerous hospital workers. He has planted seeds of goodness into this world by ignoring the comments of others who don't understand his seizures. He has planted true beauty in this world by accepting and appreciating what he has been given in this life. He waters when needed and reaps a bountiful harvest of smiles, gratitude, and goodwill for those who know him.

Landon has learned to value the simple things in his garden of life...a four-wheeler ride at dusk, a walk in the woods, a campfire on a chilly night, or an unexpected bedtime story. These are things most of us overlook. I know I do. These simple things are often too incidental for me. My life garden is often taken up with work, commitments, and bills. My garden often lacks its potential beauty because, unfortunately, I spend too much time tending the "important" things that I have planted. I water it with frustration and resentment due to overcommitment. Of course, all our gardens must have some time devoted to these other, worldly priorities. However, if I am not careful, I miss the harvest of those truly important things.

Landon notices these little, seemingly insignificant things. He makes them a priority in his life. Because of his choices, he has grown a beautiful garden. He knows when to plant and he knows when to water. He somehow has realized the kind of life garden he would have if he ignored what others call the unimportant things; the things that really matter...things like people, charitable deeds, and a generous heart. These are things many of us miss in our busy gardens of life.

I think Landon can offer all of us a few tips on planting and gardening. With care he has yielded a bountiful harvest. He observes the people in his garden. He knows when to nurture them at the right times with a smile, a wave, or a twinkle in his eye. Yes, gardening does take some effort, but perhaps it doesn't really demand as much time as I once thought. We all can plant those little seeds daily when we switch our focus to what is really of lasting value.

I had it turned around years ago when I chose to teach my son how to plant a garden. I should have had him teach me how to plant. My rows would probably have been crooked, but I would have had a deeper appreciation for the simple things in life. I would have more consistently placed people and moments above exhaustive commitments and worldly priorities Adults have a challenging time doing this.

My son is helping me learn that simplicity in life is what brings it beauty! Landon already has mastered this concept. His garden is a reflection of all that he holds dear in this life. I believe he has the makings of a master gardener.

- Appreciate the simple things in life.

CHAPTER 4:
Weeding

L.B.

You know from the last chapter that I enjoy gardening. I love the dirt in my hands. I love crawling through a row and reaching the other end with the sense of satisfaction of looking at a weed-free space. Mind you, I don't love the actual weeding, at least not the part when the tough ones with deep roots don't want to let go of their earthly homes. But weeding is a part of gardening, and it is necessary to maximize my harvest. I have learned how and when to pluck up unwanted things. Right after a gentle rain is a good time to clean up my garden. I have also learned, through the years, that if I ignore the weeds or put off the process of uprooting, they will eventually take over my garden. Even small, shallow weeds will spread until they are out of control.

This is also true in my garden of life. I am not as good at uprooting *stuff* there. I have a lot of stuff that has been growing for years in my heart. Just when I think I got it by the roots it shows itself again. Sadly, I am prone to remember the faults and offenses of others, and although I truly have tried to forgive those who have offended me, I still have not totally uprooted and thrown out those memories. Stuff takes up room in our lives. When our hearts get so crowded with stuff, we have less room for the things that truly belong there; things like generosity, compassion, forgiveness, and love...the important things we should be growing.

My son knows how to uproot. Landon does it often, and he tends the garden of his heart with a good strong hoe that takes out those negative characteristics at the root.

If anyone has a reason to be growing *stuff* in their garden of life...stuff like anger, resentment, and unforgiveness, it is Landon. From the world's view, he would be justified. His disability has robbed him of much, and others in this world who struggle like him have done just that.

Yet I constantly see him plucking away at those weeds of life. I believe that because of his struggles, he is quick to accept others. Because of his hurts, he is quick to show empathy. Because of his gratitude for life itself, he is quick to show forgiveness. In Landon's mind, life is too short to hold grudges, and he doesn't want his garden cluttered with those weeds.

I have seen him uproot reasons to be angry with other children who have ridiculed him for what they didn't realize were the results of hundreds of seizures. As a parent, I don't always want to pluck those weeds up. I have, at times, wanted to water them heavily and then send the harvest back to those kids! Many times, I have witnessed other children and sometimes even adults staring at my son. I have learned over time to ask them if they have any questions, because I truly want them to understand his disability better. But early on, I just grew upset with their stares.

During one particularly tough time in his life, Landon's salivary glands were affected by the barrage of seizures. He was unable to control his drooling. I carried a handkerchief everywhere we went and was constantly dabbing at his mouth. Landon handled the frustration of these situations admirably, even though others were gawking at him. It was humbling to watch him. When people's ignorance led to ridicule or pointing in these situations, Landon didn't take it to heart. He forgave with sincere charity and uprooted any negative feelings.

I have also seen Landon uproot resentment, which could be growing with a flourish due to his disability. This disability keeps him from driving a car, going to college, and finding employment in the same way as his peers. This disability categorizes him as not "normal." Yes, resentment could be growing in his heart. Resentment is a bitter foe in the garden of our lives. It grows into other, nastier weeds that spread. Landon is wise in his uprooting of this pest.

Finally, I have seen Landon pluck up unforgiveness toward his parents and siblings when they, too, have judged him unfairly, lashed out with words due to sleepless nights, or not understood his good intentions gone bad. For this reason, I am thankful that my son knows how to uproot, because he has shown me unconditional love and forgiveness through this exercise of weeding. He has plucked up and gotten rid of the evidence. It is erased. He chooses to see only the good in his parents, and in others.

We are all on a journey in this world. Each of us has our own disability of sorts, our trials and personal battles that haunt us. With them come the temptation to grow negativity and resentment. We all have weeding to do and sometimes it is painful, but without this process we can never really grow the qualities that positively affect those around us and make us happier people. I am so thankful that my son can uproot what needs plucking up. Because of this, his garden is one of the most beautiful ones I have ever seen.

- Don't let negativity take root in your life.

CHAPTER 5:
Gopher Hunting

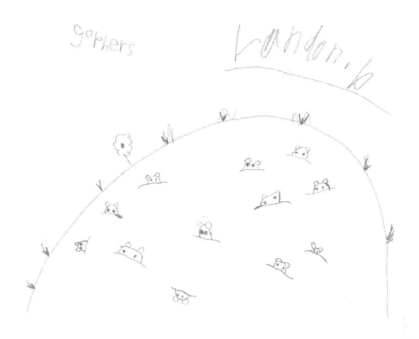

Gophers are pests! They are destructive little creatures! These rodents make holes in my yard, they dig in my garden, and they mess up my flower beds! Gophers are not my friends. When vermin mess with my property they must be stopped! Little did I know that eradicating my property of gophers would be such a fun and memorable adventure for my sons and me.

I can fondly think back to many adventures in my own childhood with my cousins and siblings. Those were times when we devised a plan and then worked together to make it happen. The memories of those times are indelibly etched into our minds and can be retrieved in a moment when we get together and start telling stories. With each telling of these stories, the details are embellished a bit more for the benefit and enjoyment of the listeners. Gopher hunting became one of those pivotal memories for my two sons.

I grew up in a hunting family. Deer hunting season came in November and was almost a dual holiday attached to Thanksgiving. Some of my brothers also hunted other game, such as partridge, ducks, and even raccoons. But nobody hunted gophers, that is, until they attacked my yard. According to my sons, "Gopher Season" was upon us!

The first gopher showed up during the summer when Landon turned seven. His health was good, and his seizures were fairly under control, at least from our standards of what constituted "under control." He and Joel were out "hunting" with their toy rifles and had just emerged from their "hunting shack," a little cedar pole cabin I had constructed for them on the wooded edge of our property. When they saw that first gopher take off across the yard, they both started yelling at the top of their lungs. I came running from the garden to see who had been obviously stung by a bee.

"Dad! We saw a gopher! A really BIG one!" Joel yelled.

"Daddy...it went down a hole right THERE!" Landon added.

After delivering all their facts to me, we began to search for more holes in the sod. After finding several more we officially declared our summer vacation to be Gopher Season.

In consideration for those readers who did not grow up in hunting families or in a rural setting, I will spare you the specific details of our exploits. However, know that we spent a good share of that summer plotting, calculating, and decimating as much of that initial gopher's family as we could. We used hoses, shovels, and a .22 rifle. There were a lot of gophers...a lot! Not a week went by that the boys and I weren't out hunting gophers. Gopher hunting could occur during meals, during campfires around the fire ring in the backyard, or during weeding time in the vegetable patch. Gopher hunting was also an acceptable reason to postpone mowing the lawn, interrupt a bike ride, or even delay bedtime. We did some of our best hunting while the boys ran around in their pajamas as the sun sank in the western sky.

Let me give it to you straight. I don't like gophers; not at all. I love most animals and can usually find at least one redemptive quality about them; however, gophers are sneaky and destructive little creatures. They multiply like rabbits. But after some thought, I was able to find one positive thing about them. Those bothersome rodents provided the best hunting experiences I will ever have with my two sons! The tales of our adventures live on, and grow, thanks to Landon's amazing storytelling.

Joel is my outdoorsman. He can outhunt me and has done so since he was thirteen years old when he shot a trophy buck that hangs on our family room wall. He has always amazed me with his knowledge of traps, snares, and weapons. He once read a library book about traps and learned how to build a mini-Burmese tiger trap! My brother next door stumbled into it one day before I even knew it existed. He hobbled up to my front door, came into the entry and asked, "How many traps does your son have out there?"

Landon, however, due to his seizures, will probably never be a hunter. Loaded rifles and deer stands don't mix with a disability that comes unexpectedly and attacks without warning. Landon has learned to be content with just helping be my eyes when we hunt together. Truly, he would be an amazing hunter with his eyesight and his skill in observation.

Because of this fact, I am thankful for those little gophers that staged an onslaught of my property during the summer of 2002. They allowed the three men of the family to hunt together. It was a summer-long safari for us. We strategized, we chased, we posted, and we succeeded. Those were hunting adventures that we will never forget. Though none of those gophers became mounts on our wall, Landon will continue to share the stories of our tactical feats for years to come, with the customary embellishments to the stories, of course!

Most of us get to enjoy childhood, at least for several years. Our adventures as children become treasured memories and help to shape us into the adults we eventually become. Landon's childhood, however, was somewhat stolen from him with hospitalizations, heavy medications along with their side effects, and frequent periods of recovery due to hundreds of seizures. The attack of seizures put much of his childhood on hold. But that summer, he got to be a "normal" country kid, and he loved every minute of it!

The summer of 2002 was not just gopher season. It was a time when two little boys got to make memories with their daddy. It was a time when an older brother "got his little brother back," albeit for just a season, without the constant threat of seizures. It was a time for which I will be forever thankful. When I think of a time to kill, I will always think of gopher hunting with my boys. How wonderful it must have felt for Landon to just be a regular kid for that one, glorious summer!

- Be a kid today. Do something just for fun.

CHAPTER 6:
Broken Bones and Heaven

Landon,

Broken bones are a pain...literally and figuratively. As a child growing up on a farm, I never broke a bone. Amazingly, the only broken bone of all seven children in my family was a nose, and that was my oldest brother while wrestling in physical education class. I did break a toe the week of my high school graduation. At our class picnic, I was standing on a big boulder in a river and tried to kick water at someone. I kicked the rock instead.

Broken bones never come at a convenient time. We never really have a period of four to six weeks when we can pencil in a broken bone because it will work in nicely with our schedule. But broken bones happen, and we deal with them, and they eventually heal. All of my children have broken a bone at least once or twice.

I remember Landon's first broken bone. He was riding his bike on the driveway. He had only been riding without training wheels for a few weeks. He suddenly had a seizure and fell off his bike. The landing was seemingly soft and yet, after complaining about his shoulder hurting, we took him to the doctor. It was a broken collarbone...the first of several breaks he would experience.

Landon has also required stitches a time or two. I remember the first time he needed them. It was right after his seizures had started. He had been playing in the family room and twirled himself dizzy, right into the corner of the television. He bled a lot, and when we got to the ER the doctor decided to just "glue him back together" rather than stitch. My wife and I found it ironically humorous when the doctor warned us to "...watch for seizures as it was a head injury."

Things get broken in this life. Bones need mending, bodies need stitching, and sometimes heads need gluing.

But not everything heals like we want it to heal. For many years Krista and I waited for Landon to be healed of his seizures. We prayed for this miracle. We longed for it. At times, when the answer didn't come, I even questioned the effectiveness of prayer or why we even put forth the effort to pray. Those were dark times for me. For you see, as a father it was my job to protect my son, and I did this to the best of my ability. But seizures were a foe that I couldn't understand. I never knew when or where they would strike, and I felt completely disabled to do my job as protector. I don't like when things can't be fixed. I don't like when healing doesn't happen.

Many nights I would sit on Landon's bed and watch him sleep. The words to a song would often run through my head. The lyrics spoke of a father asking for his son to be healed, how he dreamed of the boy he could be, and questioned if God was really listening. The phrase that always choked me up was "...if You can hear me, let me take his place somehow. See, he's not just anyone...he's my son." ("He's My Son" released in 2000 by Mark Schultz)

One night, as I sat by Landon's bedside after an exceptionally long seizure, the chorus of that song haunted me once again. Landon looked up at me and attempted to speak. After a seizure, his words were often garbled and unintelligible, but they were unmistakable this time. He looked into my eyes and declared, "Dad...I know God will heal me someday, even if it's when I get to heaven." My heart broke and I wept openly as I held my son...my son whose faith was paramount to mine.

Oftentimes we are so busy waiting for relief on this earth that we forget the eternal perspective. My son, in his fragile state, gave me a reminder that night, and I held him for a long time as he fell asleep in my arms.

Suddenly all my questions about prayer seemed insignificant. Sometimes we don't have all the answers, and we are asked to just accept where we are in this life. It is all about having child-like faith. Landon had this faith, and his convictions encouraged my faltering heart.

I still spend time thinking about Landon being healed on this earth. I continue to pray about it. I dream of what he could be doing if he didn't have seizures and of the possibilities and opportunities that would open for him if he would wake up one morning and the disability would just be gone. These are good things to ponder. Dreams of miracles are what give us hope and help us persevere.

But I love who my son is, seizures and all, and I realize that his disability has helped shape him into an incredible and thoughtful young man with a strong faith. Healing is a good thing. Truly, it is a remarkable thing, but I have reached a place in life where I can be content with where we are as a family. We have struggled, and we have grown as people. Our relationships have gained depth because of what we have endured together. Along with Landon, we dream together of the future.

I am thankful for those dreams...the ones where my son can look forward to the day when he truly will be healed with no limitations. That is a day we can all look forward to with no more seizures, no more broken bones, and no more heartaches. A time to heal...a time for miracles. Landon and I await that day!

- Trust and believe with child-like faith.

CHAPTER 7:
Home Repairs

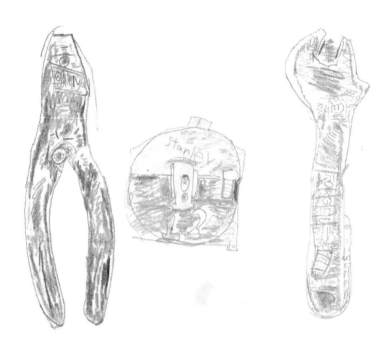

I am not a handyman. I want to be, but I am not. I want to build amazing furniture. I want to be skilled in woodworking. I want a shop of power tools along with the ability to adeptly use all of them. I want to be able to fix things when they need repairing. But that is not who I am. Those are not the strengths I possess.

When things need repairing at our house, I do my best. Sometimes I can even impress myself when I figure things out. I have learned to troubleshoot to fix some things. But usually I pray that it won't have to be looked at again for fear someone else will actually see how I "fixed" it.

In my life, I have helped tear down many things. I have torn down sheds, fences, scenery, and classrooms. Tearing down is faster and easier than building. It usually doesn't require an intense plan or strategy. I am good at tearing down. It can even be enjoyable.

Landon likes to tear down. Over the years he has dismantled the organization of my garage on several occasions. He has "taken apart" his bedroom, his bookshelves, and even spaces in our house occupied by others. Some of his best work of tearing down has happened in the wee hours of the morning when his unsuspecting family is still asleep.

When Landon was about twelve years old, he was struggling with sleepless nights. He has periodically struggled with this over the years, but during this time it was an excessive problem. Whether this was due to seizure activity or interactions of his medication, my wife and I were often fearful of what he might do during the night while the rest of us slept. We had a monitor in his room, but if he was extremely quiet, he could remain undetected by sleeping parents. Typically, if he awoke during the night and couldn't sleep, he would look at books, draw a picture, or do something quietly in his room. Other times we were not as lucky, and he would occasionally turn on lights, music, or televisions as he roamed the house. One time he went outside for a bike ride in the darkness of the pre-dawn morning.

On one particular night during this time, Landon demonstrated his great ability to tear down. I woke up at about 3 a.m. and had a peculiar feeling. I went to Landon's room to check on him, but he wasn't there. The house was bathed in darkness. Before panic set in I looked through the basement. I noticed a light under the closed door of the downstairs bathroom. As I slowly opened the door, I found Landon with his screwdriver in hand. The entire vanity...doors, handles, everything ...had been taken apart. He had fallen asleep on the floor after this project was completed. Amusement, relief, frustration, and sleepiness converged in me as I gently woke him and very pointedly sent him back to bed. Incidentally, we have since purchased a monitor that not only allows us to HEAR what he is doing but also to SEE what he is doing!

Sometimes the process of tearing down is planned. Other times when people tear things down others don't appreciate the effort they have put into the activity. Tearing down can be destructive. Tearing down can be purposeful. Sometimes it even causes pain.

Over the years Landon has helped me tear down other things in my "house." I have had to break down my defenses. I have had to reacquaint myself with thinking as a child and accepting things as they are. I have had to tear down expectations of my son, realizing that I have absolutely no idea what it is like to live daily with a seizure disorder and the injury it has caused to his brain over the years. I have found this type of tearing down to be much more difficult than the physical act. Fortunately,

Landon doesn't help me tear down like a foreman would at a demolition site. He does it quietly and over time, with complete acceptance of my inadequacy to master the task, especially in the initial stages.

Landon has also helped me tear down walls of judgment that can so often and so easily creep into my character. Having a son who faces challenges has helped me accept those who are different than I, even when I don't understand. It has helped me develop empathy for others. It has made me a more compassionate teacher working with children in my classroom who struggle with learning and developmental disabilities. It has helped me understand that we never truly understand another's motives until we have walked in their shoes and dealt with their challenges in life.

There is a time for tearing down. In those times I remember that not everything is perfect in this world. Walking through those times helps me admit that not everything is right in my life either. Times of tearing down can be painful, but they can also bring good changes to the people we are. For all of this, I am truly thankful to my son, the one who has often demonstrated to me that there is a time to tear down.

- Believe the best about others.

CHAPTER 8:
It Takes a Community

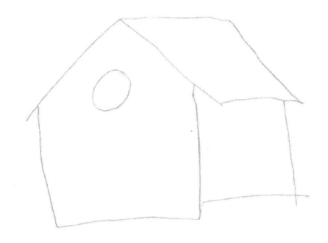

Landon

When we built our house in 1995, I vowed never to undertake something like that again. Building a house is mentally taxing, physically exhausting, and time consuming. It takes hours of planning and anguishing over designs, choices of colors, flooring, and lighting. My father-in-law is a contractor, and he built our house, with the help of members of both of our families. I am thankful to him for the house that has been our home for these past 23 years.

Since that time, I have realized that there is another type of building we are called to do. It is one that also requires time, personal sacrifice, and a commitment that far outweighs the building of a house. It is the building up of others.

Affirmation goes a long way in this world. We all need it, and we all desire it. It feels good. Because of the toll seizures have taken on his body, Landon's left side doesn't always work so well. It is difficult for him to confidently perform tasks that require both hands. Even with reminders and stretching exercises it remains a challenge. Tying shoes, buckling a belt, and many other daily activities that we take for granted have been burdensome for him at times. That is why I have appreciated the people who have taken the time to work with Landon and to build him up. Three of these people stand out in my mind.

Spike was a retired man in our community. He was a friend of the principal of the elementary school where I worked. Spike had a heart of gold. He had a quick and easy smile. Spike had a bit of time to volunteer at our school. For one year he did woodworking with Landon. Knowing how Landon dreamt of being a carpenter, Spike helped make this partially a reality. Landon learned to measure wood, cut it with supervision, sand it, and turn it into a beautiful project. Landon looked forward to his weekly visits with Spike. Sometimes, due to seizures, Landon was too tired to build something with Spike, so on those days Spike read with him and built in other ways. These precious times meant the world to Landon.

In that year Landon made numerous bird houses and bird feeders. He could have done this with his parents or other family members if we had taken the time, but Spike was someone outside of Landon's circle. He gave the time to invest in a life...a life of a young man who would forever remember that dedication, commitment, and those weekly visits. Many of those bird houses were given away as gifts. Whenever I see one, I remember that there is a time to build. Spike was a man who built Landon up.

Jim was a former teacher of visually-impaired children. After 30 years of teaching, he and his minister wife ended up in our small community for just a year. This happened to be Landon's last year in high school. Because of a long hospitalization the summer before, we had few plans for this final year of schooling. We were lacking a job coach for his out-of-school work experiences. Two days before school started Jim called our principal and introduced himself. He explained that he didn't want to substitute teach, but only wanted to volunteer to work with someone that needed him. He wanted "to make a difference." Jim made a difference!

After many years of demands on his professional life, Jim was worn. He was looking for perspective. When people asked me where Jim came from, I responded, "Heaven opened up and dropped him down." This man invested and affirmed abilities in Landon that nobody outside his family had ever done. He daily gave Landon positive feedback on his work ethic and the progress he saw developing in his jobs. He worked side by side, listened to Landon's endless stories, and shared life with my son. He became a true friend. As much as we were grateful to Jim, he always echoed our feelings by telling us how much his life had been changed and enriched by Landon's presence. I told Jim one day what a blessing he was to our family. He smiled, pointed at Landon and responded, "He's the blessing!"

The impact Jim had on Landon changed our direction for his post-high school years. Jim had significant input at Landon's IEP (Individualized Education Program) meetings at school that year. He encouraged Landon to try new things. He helped pave the way for Landon's first job at the sheltered workshop where he continues to work today. Jim was a life-changer. Jim was an angel in disguise. Jim was a man who built Landon up.

At the end of the school year, we knew that Jim would be moving. The thought of finding a new job coach who could match Jim's quality and care seemed impossible. Then Paula entered the scene.

Paula worked at the sheltered workshop where Landon found employment, which started right after Landon got out of school in June. Over the course of time, Paula developed a relationship with Landon, affirming him in a way similar to Jim. As we watched their work relationship develop, we noticed some of the same qualities we had seen in Jim. Paula was quick to smile. She appreciated Landon's stories. She had a way of sharing life with him.

She helped Landon develop a resume which led to another part-time job doing accommodations work at a local camp. Paula's commitment and dedication were evident each Friday afternoon as she worked side by side with Landon at Forest Springs. Weekly she gave us amazing and encouraging reports about the growth she was seeing each time they worked together. Our hearts were touched as she told us about his amazing work ethic and initiative. Her words, "I look forward to my time with Landon" were like a balm to us. For years we had wondered what Landon would do after high school. Paula was making employment not only an opportunity, but also an enjoyable reality. With her guidance and encouragement, she helped Landon secure another part-time job in our local grocery store. We saw Landon's skills and stamina continually increase in his work. Paula was a woman who built Landon up. She continues to work with him today, building him up and impacting his life greatly.

There is a time for building and for building up. As Landon was being built up, he, in turn, built others up. We will be forever grateful to Spike, Jim, and Paula who all came along at specific times and invested in Landon's life. But each of them also related to us how Landon encouraged and challenged them in their own lives during their time with him. This was no surprise to me as Landon has always been a great affirmer. Perhaps his challenges in life prompt him to build others up as he sees the importance of it. Landon is one of the few people I know who rarely disrespects people with his comments. He often leaves people feeling better about themselves.

Along our journey in life we encounter people who are builders. They invest and enrich our walk and find ways to encourage us along the way. Their affirmation has the power to change us and, in so doing, change those around us. Landon has always dreamed of becoming a carpenter...a builder. I am thinking that he was born to do this type of building. He is a builder of people, which is perhaps the most important job in our world. When I think of a time to build, I think of my son and I smile.

- Thank someone who has invested in your life.

CHAPTER 9:
Breaking Down

Landon

I am a man in touch with my emotions. I can admit that.
When issues hit, they hit me hard. My wife once said of
me that I was "...a glass half-empty kind of guy." She
didn't mean it in a bad way. She knows I have my "up"
moments, too. But I am a realist, and I don't always
expect things to work out perfectly. This is precisely why
a seizure-disorder interrupting life is rough on me. I have
occasionally been known to weep. Oh sure, I cry while
watching a movie when the faithful dog returns home or
the soldier makes it home for Christmas, but I can just as
quickly get over it. However, over the years of dealing
with seizures, my times of weeping have not been as
easy to overcome.

Landon had brain mapping surgery in November of
2005. Many factors that played into this surgery brought
me to the depths of my emotions. We were separated
from our other three children over Thanksgiving. That
was difficult. I had to prepare to be gone from school for
three weeks. That was difficult. But the biggest obstacle
to tackle was the actual day to day life in a hospital far
from home seeking answers, consulting with surgeons,
and then the actual surgery. Knowing they were going to
put my ten-year-old son to sleep, while he was already
on fragile ground, and then cut open his head to explore
the origin of his seizures was an overwhelming prospect.
However, it was a step in a direction we had not yet
taken. We had been advised by our neurologist back
home that this was our next and best option. It was a
difficult decision to make, and it involved two separate
trips to Cleveland, Ohio, thirteen hours from our home.

The day of the surgery I wanted to be strong for Landon
and for my wife. We were alone in a faraway city and we
were facing a surgical procedure that would take several
hours. The procedure would help us determine our son's
future, and we were scared. As we said goodbye when

they wheeled him off to surgery, he cried out to me in a way he had never done before.

Landon had always had a high pain tolerance. For the previous six years he had basically accepted his seizures as a way of life. But on that morning, he grabbed my hand, looked into my eyes, and said, "Daddy, don't ever leave me." This was almost more than I could take. As they took him out the door and down the hall I collapsed in a chair and wept. This was the first time I remembered Landon breaking down.

Five long hours later, as Landon was wheeled back into the recovery room, my eyes took in more than my mind was able. A tube coming out of his bandaged head was draining more blood than I could have imagined. We had already talked to the surgeon who gave us the unfortunate news that the mapping confirmed further surgeries would not be helpful. In fact, they could make things worse. We watched him lie in the bed, we looked at the monitors for signs of his awakening, and we watched that blood flow down the tube from his skull and into the collection site. We had not signed up for this. What had we done?

After about an hour of waiting, the phone in the room suddenly rang. I answered it and immediately broke down. A friend from home called to see how we were doing AND to tell us that she and her family were leaving in a day to drive 13 hours to spend Thanksgiving with us. Hardly able to talk, I relayed the news to Krista. More weeping...more emotion...more breaking down.

Breaking down is humbling for a man. Crying in front of friends is not comfortable for me. Weeping in front of strangers is awkward. But there are times to break down. Over the 16 days that we were at Cleveland Clinic, we broke down many times. On the way back home to Wisconsin, we broke down many more. This trip was going to be our answer, the answer to the problem that we had tried so many other ways to solve, all without the results that we were seeking. Our anticipated journey home had been one of victory and relief before the surgery. Now we would face the prospect of what to do next. Seeing the stitches that would soon turn to scars and the bandages on my son's head caused me to question why we had ever considered this surgery in the first place.

After arriving home, we attempted to pick up the pieces and go on with life. With Christmas right around the corner, we rallied to make the holiday special for our children. But after Christmas, we hit another dark place. It was a somber place that lasted several months. Krista and I both experienced depression in our own ways. We experienced times of weeping weekly, if not daily. Through all this time after arriving back home, Landon remained strong and accepting of our new reality. In many ways, he became even more of a hero to me.

I did a lot of self-reflection that winter...about life...and choices...and how we don't always get what we want in this life. That's not how prayer works. We don't just put in our order and receive exactly what we desire. If that were the case, we would never know how to wait, we would never grow as people, and we wouldn't have a faith that was worth much. I thought about how, during those times of breaking down, we reach out for something. Krista and I reached out for God, and we found His presence through all that we experienced. That didn't mean that our journey suddenly became easy. But our faith and Landon's faith somehow grew over that period of months in ways we couldn't have imagined. We reached out for answers. When we couldn't find them, we accepted that sometimes the answers just aren't there, at least for the moment...but God is.

In my estimation, life is better and so much more enjoyable when things go smoothly. Yet without the valleys in this life, would we appreciate the mountain tops as much? We have traveled many valleys with Landon over the years. Some have been brief routes, but others have lasted for long and arduous months.

We have also had some amazing times on the top of the mountain. The valleys bring us closer to our Heavenly Father as we reach out for His strength to endure. The mountains help us appreciate Him and His gifts to us in this life.

I learned during those months after Landon's surgery that there are times in life when we break down. I learned that there are times in our seasons of life when we weep. It is who we are. It is how we were designed. It is our crying out to our Maker. I also was reminded that we are not alone in these journeys. In those moments of weeping if we are listening carefully, we can hear His voice assuring us that He is still there.

- Rely on others who love and support you.

Emotions can be difficult to navigate. I find them interesting; even ironic. One minute we can be crying and the next we are laughing uncontrollably. In an instant, anger can turn into resolution and selfishness into generosity. Psychologists have studied human emotions for years, books have been written about them, and drugs have been developed to control them. But can anyone fully understand human emotions? I have decided not to obsess about my flimsy grasp of them. Instead, I am thankful that they travel so closely together. One emotion is always just a step away from its counter-emotion. To me that means that after our times of weeping, we can often find laughter and joy soon to follow.

Landon has an amazing memory. He also has an uncanny sense of timing in delivering lines he has rehearsed from television shows and movies. He would make a great comedian. (Perhaps we'll pursue that road together when I finish this book!) Even in his early years he had people laughing with his quotes. One afternoon, while sitting down for a picnic lunch at a large family reunion, he looked at several people he had never met before who happened to be at his table. He held up his glass of lemonade and asked, "Is this safe to drink? It looks unsanitary!" Some at the table recognized the line immediately from a current children's movie. Others just thought my son had an amazing wit for a four-year-old.

Landon also loves to quote movie lines while he is working. I think it keeps him going as he faces tasks one might find monotonous. One day, while working with his job coach, Paula, he yelled out, "Get me those puppies!" in his best Cruella DeVille voice. He nearly gave Paula a heart attack.

Landon loves to laugh when he watches movies. He has a hearty shriek of a guffaw, which is unmistakably his trademark laugh. When you hear it, you know he is in full enjoyment of the moment. Landon never watches a movie just once, nor even twice. For Landon a movie becomes a part of his repertoire, and he watches it repeatedly to get the right timing and inflection in the lines he memorizes.

Some of Landon's favorite things to watch that make him laugh are old episodes of "The Andy Griffith Show." Barney Fife has become one of Landon's heroes over the years. He has Barney's walk down, as well as his voice and his mannerisms. As a parent I have found this humorous at times, and other times it can be just plain annoying. It's not easy to dole out a consequence to someone like Barney.

Landon loves to recall entire episodes of the show to doctors, people in stores, or basically anyone who seems interested enough to listen. Barney has brought much laughter to Landon in this world. For that reason, I am thankful to Mr. Fife, despite his irritating personality.

The most interesting thing I find about Landon's laughter is that there are no rules or boundaries about when it can appear. I am much more selective about the times when my laughter emerges. I try to follow unwritten social mandates about when and where laughter is appropriate. Landon's hearty laugh appears when it wants...right after long nights of seizures, during quiet and tense medical moments, or even during church services. Laughter is a unique thing. It demands a response from others in the room. In most cases people enjoy Landon's laughter. His enjoyment of life, his love of humor, and his laughter have helped others cope with HIS situation. His laughter has brought healing to those around him. I find it amazing that the young man with the disability has brought healing to those with whom he comes in contact.

There is no ignoring Landon's laugh, and it is a laugh that can bring joy to those who hear it.

King Solomon said there is a time to laugh. He also said that a joyful heart is good medicine. As we have walked Landon through surgery and medical procedures his laughter has still been with us. When we have dealt with strict diets and numerous med changes his laughter could still be heard.

I believe that Landon has found a type of therapy to help him deal with his disability. He has chosen the therapy of laughter. He loves to laugh, and he loves to have others laugh with him. If you ask Landon the best time for laughter, I believe he would answer with a hearty guffaw, "Anytime!"

- Laugh heartily every day.

CHAPTER 11:
Saying Goodbye

Saying goodbye was never easy for me. As the youngest of seven children I struggled with saying goodbye to my older siblings at the end of weekends and holidays as they headed back to college. Saying goodbye to lost pets or friends who moved away was also difficult for me. My best friend in grade school moved across the state in third grade. It was traumatic.

As a child, I don't remember attending funerals. Three of my grandparents had already passed away by the time I was born. During those growing up years I do not recall losing someone close to me. I was fortunate, yet I didn't really have a clear concept of mourning the loss of someone I held dear. This, of course, changed when I became an adult.

When Landon was two years old my father died suddenly. He had been diagnosed with congestive heart failure, yet his departure from this earth was still somewhat unexpected by our family and it took me by surprise. It was Christmas Eve, 1997. That morning, as I performed CPR on my dad with my mother at my side, I realized I was completely unprepared to face the loss of him.

I actively mourned my father's death for many months. It was emotionally difficult to face the reality that my children would only know my dad through stories and memories I shared with them. My daughters were not even born yet. Joel and Landon were both so young that I knew they would only have vague impressions of him in their memory banks. My dad had called Landon "Bright Eyes" since his birth. This nickname stuck for many years, possibly in part, as my way of holding onto a piece of my father.

Grief and mourning are difficult concepts to understand. I believe that grief never fully goes away. It dulls over time however, it forever changes life on this earth as it creates a hole where a loved one formerly lived. Mourning is the process of accepting grief and the changes it brings. I mourned the fact that my dad would never attend school programs for my children, take them for rides in his truck or on his four-wheeler, or invest in their lives as other grandpas did for their grandchildren. Because of his age, Landon, of course, did not mourn my father's death. I found that having young children in my life at a time of loss was a blessing. Their daily needs forced me to have a sort of resiliency and kept me going through the stages of grief.

Two days before Landon's 18th birthday, my mom left this earth. She was surrounded in her hospital bed by all seven of her children, their spouses, and most of her 25 grandchildren, as well as several great-grandchildren. She was 87 years old, and even though we knew we would see her again someday, we were still not prepared to have her leave. Once again, we mourned as a family, but this time with my children as active participants.

We mourned the loss of an amazing woman whose love showed through her daily life in so many ways. We mourned the loss of Grandma's support and presence in our lives through all the years of seizures. She had accompanied us on our very first trip to Cleveland for our consultation. We mourned that she would not see Landon graduate from high school the following spring. We mourned the loss of her intuitive heart causing her to show up at our door at just the right time when we felt we couldn't go on during a rough bout with seizures. We mourned that the dearest of women on this earth would no longer be right next door. The days of walking to her farm, opening the door, and smelling her sweet rolls baking were now in the past.

Another type of mourning I have experienced during my lifetime is for Landon. It is an ongoing one which I have tried to keep somewhat silent and hidden from others, but one that I attempt to share only with my wife when the words that accompany my emotions cannot be silenced. It is a mourning that I know she shares with me.

Since the onset of his seizures, we have jointly mourned the loss of his childhood and the loss of dreams. We have mourned Landon's loss of life decisions, such as attending college, choosing a career, and starting his own family. While others his age have planned their future, we have mourned his loss of abilities to make his own financial decisions or feel the excitement of setting and determining the course for his own life.

Mourning, grieving, and weeping are active ways that we outwardly show our sorrow in this world. I have done all of these in my lifetime. I did them when I lost my parents, and I have done them over the years as I faced a disability that is, quite simply, unfair and robs my son of his independence.

Mourning is painful and sometimes difficult, yet if it does its job, it eventually helps bring us to the next place... acceptance. In Landon's case, it has brought him beyond that to a place of contentment. Although Krista and I sometimes continue to mourn for those activities and experiences of life that he will probably never know personally, he has shown an unnatural ability to accept his circumstances and live in a world of happiness, satisfaction, and peace. He refuses to get stuck in the stages of mourning. When disappointment attacks him, he processes, grieves, and then moves on to enjoy what life does have to offer.

Grief and mourning are realities of this life. We will all face them eventually, in some way. They change our lives and the process can be long. The pathways that they take us down are somewhat unique as we each face them in our own way and in our own time. It is painful and seemingly never-ending in the beginning. It not only changes us, but it also changes those around us and our relationships with them.

I am thankful that my son has shown me how to mourn things responsibly in this life and how to move beyond my present circumstances. It is a lesson I am still learning. His ability to do this has brought contentment to his own life and modeled that quality for me. He has demonstrated joy amidst the sorrow and hope amidst the mourning. He has brought gratitude to others, like me, who have observed the process. Landon mourns, but he doesn't stay there. He has shown me that a time to mourn precedes acceptance and a time to move on.

- Take a moment to remember a loss you have mourned. Reflect on where that process has taken you.

CHAPTER 12:
Learning to Dance in Rainstorms

In our bedroom hangs a large print of a famous painting called "The Singing Butler." When Krista and I first saw it in an art gallery, we were emotionally moved. We stared in silence at it for many minutes, both realizing how much it embodied our lives. It is a painting of a finely dressed couple on the shore of an ocean. With the threatening clouds of a squall overhead, they are dancing in the rainstorm. His butler is holding an umbrella over their heads, and her maid is standing nearby holding a parasol. It spoke to us of the support we had often felt from others through the storms of our lives. Within the next year I found and purchased an affordable print of this amazing work of art for Krista's birthday...the one that now graces our home.

The following Christmas I gave Krista a decorative wooden plate with the phrase "Life isn't about waiting for the storm to pass. It's about learning to dance in the rain." It seemed to also capture, as the painting had, what had become a mantra of our lives. Along with it, I gave her a gift of dance lessons for the two of us. I am not a dancer. I have no good moves on the dance floor. I am awkward and uncomfortable as a dancer, but I knew this gift would really touch my wife. It did...she cried. Mission accomplished!

So, we took ballroom dancing lessons. For the better part of six months we went to dance classes together. Surprisingly, it was fun! More surprisingly, I found some moves. We even had moments when we thought that we actually looked good on the dance floor. Since that time, we have enjoyed dancing at weddings...in our living room...and even on our deck. Dancing brings us together. Dancing momentarily takes us away from our troubles. We can now call ourselves dancers.

As I reflect on our married life together, much of the time has included dealing with Landon's seizures and related challenges. In retrospect, I believe we have been dancing for a long, long time. We have danced through long nights with a dance that looked like an embrace. We have danced through anxious medical appointments with a dance that appeared as hand-holding. We have danced through missed family events and planned getaways that suddenly got cancelled due to seizure activity with a dance that simply resembled being close. We have even danced through brain surgery and its recovery with a dance that looked exactly like prayer.

Dancing usually requires only two people. But I have found over the years that most of our dancing in the rain has been accompanied by a circle of family and friends. Since the onset of Landon's seizures, we have been supported by hundreds of people who have faithfully prayed for us. Some pray weekly...others pray when we come to mind. Several have committed to lifting us up to our Heavenly Father daily. This has greatly humbled and affected us over the years.

These amazing people have joined our dance, each in their own way. Some provided the music as they sat with us in silence waiting for answers or for a night of seizures to end. Some provided the beat as they helped us "keep on" with life when we just felt like we couldn't go on. Some cleared the dance floor for us as they graciously offered to stay with Landon, so we could get away for some much-needed respite. Still others brought refreshments as they met needs in our lives and prayed for the survival of our marriage. Without these dance partners, I'm not sure where we would be today as a family. Their support humbles me to a level of gratitude that I cannot fully express.

Landon occasionally dances...at weddings, community events, or special occasions. One time at a quinceanera he was the first one in line to dance with the special, young lady after she danced with her father. He has also square danced at a barn dance held each spring in our neighborhood. I have a very special memory of him dancing with my mom at one of our last family weddings before she died. It is a priceless remembrance...one I will never forget! Landon looks like his father on the dance floor. He could definitely use a few lessons, but he enjoys himself thoroughly.

As I grow older, I have realized that Landon has been a dancer his entire life. Through all the hospitalizations, long nights, disappointments, lonely days, and crushed dreams...he has gracefully danced his way through all these storms. He has not waited for the storm to pass, but he has continued to emotionally dance through it, reaching out his hand to those who would join his dance...a dance that would lift their spirits if they would just follow his lead.

Someday I hope to be a "great dancer" like my son. I am learning more each year about how to do this. However, I am still not the dancer Landon is. I aspire to be an accomplished dancer like him...one that is so immersed in the dance that I can shut out the storm pounding on my door.

When Krista and I took dancing lessons we had to search for an instructor and a location that offered them. We should have looked right in our own house. Fred Astaire was there all the time!

- Dance in the rain, even when it is difficult.

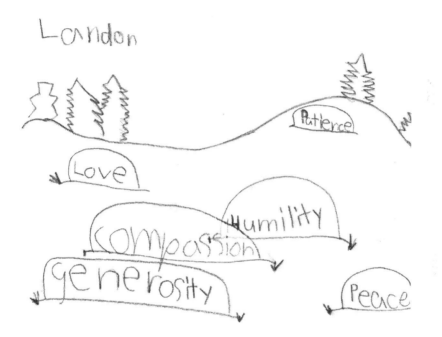

My dad was a generous man. Although not worldly wealthy, he was rich in family and friends. He was rich in character and work ethic. These qualities gained him respect in this world. He was a man who would help anyone if he could. Many times, during my growing up years we had guests in the house we had never met before. My mom used to say, "Most people bring home stray animals...Wyllie brings home stray people." It was true. Hitchhikers, people out of work, all types ended up on our farm...to figure things out. My mom was also generous and supportive of this arrangement. They invested in many lives over the years in ways that we could not imagine.

I strive to be a generous man. I would like to think that I am like my dad. He modeled charity of time and resources. I try to do the same. I find it fulfilling to help people who are hurting in my world, and I hope that I have passed that trait on to my children. Generosity breeds joy in our lives.

Scattering stones, as Solomon called it, could be defined as many things. The stones of altars being taken down... sheep gates made of stones and scattered...these are just a few ideas. When I think of scattering stones, I think of precious stones or jewels. I like to think that scattering stones is doing what we can to make this world a better place.

Whenever I have taken my classes on a field trip, one of our mottos is to leave the place better than we found it. This is a great credo of life. By modeling this behavior, it becomes easier for my students to follow. It helps us do our part to make things better in this world. I like to think the same about people. Leave them better than we found them. That is true generosity.

Landon has a generous heart like my father. I once saw him drop over 70 dollars in the offering plate at church. He was just a young boy, and it was the day after his birthday. He decided to give every bit of the money he had received for a better cause than spending it on himself. Landon doesn't value money as a priority in his life. People are more important. He doesn't strive to gain worldly wealth. In many ways, he doesn't fully understand money or prosperity. Landon believes that he is rich, and I would have to agree. His life is full of people who love and support him. He desires to be equally generous to those around him with kindness that comes from a truly wealthy heart.

Landon has shown me through the years that scattering stones gets easier the longer you do it. My dad did the same thing. Whether we are scattering financially, emotionally, or physically with our time, there is something very satisfying about scattering generosity. When we hold tightly to our worldly goods, it is difficult to share them. A tight, miserly grasp cannot effectively scatter anything. It is also accompanied by suspicion, mistrust, and fear. When we release our hold on things and open ourselves to the support of others, we find the world a much richer place.

The stones Solomon spoke of scattering may have been rubies, emeralds, or other precious gems. Though beautiful and costly, these gems have no eternal value. Solomon was a wealthy man and was undoubtedly called upon many times to be generous. But we don't have to be wealthy to scatter stones. The stones of real value in this world are the ones we can scatter daily. It takes an effort of our will but ends up blessing others as well as ourselves. These are the stones of humility, compassion, peace, patience, and love. Scattering them takes a bit of practice and often a bit more time, but it becomes habit forming and eventually leads to a way of life.

I have watched the character trait of generosity develop in my son over the years. We have worked together on this. It takes a willing spirit and a caring heart. Landon has learned to scatter stones. Scattering stones makes his world a better place. It makes a difference in the lives of others. My dad would be proud of his grandson!

- Demonstrate heartfelt generosity in some way today.

CHAPTER 14:
Rare Finds

My great-grandfather was a gatherer of stones in the true sense of the word. He built bridges in the mountains of Sweden before he and his young family emigrated to the United States in the late 1800s. After settling in northern Wisconsin, he built a stone bridge in the small town near where I was raised. Those gathered stones are a tribute to him and to the spirit of many pioneers of long ago.

This world is full of collectors. I believe that they gather stones in their own way. I have, at times during my life, collected things...coins, old bottles, and antiques. I love watching shows where people bring their old treasures or collections and find them worth thousands of dollars. I have seen tough, old army veterans and little old ladies break down on these shows as they realize the value of their possessions. Collecting can be a valuable hobby.

Collectors are observant...they are always on the lookout for an addition to their collection. They sometimes find it in the oddest of places. I once found an old Mercury Dime while digging out weeds in my mom's flower bed. Years ago, my aunt lost my grandma's wedding ring while she was playing with it. She was a young girl at the time. 18 years later it was found while excavating some dirt on the complete opposite side of the house where it was lost. As a young boy, I found some Buffalo head nickels at a garage sale for less than a dollar and bought them all.

Collectors are into rare finds. They have an eye for them. They seem to know what they are looking for. I like to think of myself as a collector. I like to think that I have an eye for the rare find. My rare finds are not always worth monetary value, but I take great pleasure in them. I have enjoyed many rare finds along this journey of life. When our collector eyes are open to them, we can find them in the most unusual places.

Walking through the woods on a spring morning and finding an apple tree in full blossom in a place where no apple tree should be growing...that is a rare find. Looking out the window after a rainstorm to find a beautiful double rainbow, incapable of finding the exact words to describe it...that is a rare find. Driving along a rural highway and seeing a young fawn nursing while the doe patiently nibbles grass...that, too, is a rare find. I have realized that when I am privileged with those rare finds in life, I grow more appreciative of life.

But back to those monetary finds...the ones that make people rich on antique shows. I tend to think many of my finds are valuable, even when they aren't. Furthermore, because I am a first-grade teacher, I am a saver. I never know when I might need the very thing that I was tempted to throw out. There is a fine line between being a collector and a hoarder. My wife has tried to help me see that line for the past 28 years, not with complete success, I must admit.

Landon is a collector...a gatherer...a gatherer of beauty and rarities. He is observant, far beyond the average person, and he finds great satisfaction in those little things in life. Each day he collects and gathers moments, happenings, and sights and then relives them in his mind throughout the next few hours or even days. His memory is an amazing thing, and he can retrieve each of these treasures in a heartbeat.

When Landon gathers stones, he gathers them in his mind. But he is always ready to share them with another. I have learned to appreciate these stones, and I believe it has helped me look for the stones of this world; the ones I can gather together in a warm and comfort-filled spot in my memories.

Landon has helped me gather so many things over the years. I may have missed these things had it not been for him. Together we have gathered sunsets…the amazing ones that fill the entire sky with so many shades of brilliant color that it seems unreal. Together we have gathered sights of wildlife…an eagle flying overhead, a newly hatched baby turtle crawling to the nearest water, and more bears and deer than we can count. Together we have gathered clouds…the puffy, white ones that start like cotton candy but turn into horses and chariots and buildings. We have also gathered the dark, threatening kinds that swirl in the sky and turn green and gray at the same time.

Most of what Landon and I have gathered together we hold safely in our minds. They are not stones that will make either of us wealthy, but they have a richness all their own. They bring life true meaning as they bring the two of us together.

Landon sees things I miss. His DISABILITY has given him an ABILITY to observe. I would love to see the world through Landon's eyes without the effort it takes. He helps me do this at times, but apart from him I am back to my own tunnel vision. He observes the world as a beautiful place, full of wonder and experiences to see, to appreciate, and to remember. I think these are the stones Solomon was referring to when he said there was a time to gather stones. I am so thankful to my son, the stone-gatherer, who daily helps me see the world as it should be seen…a wonderful place God has given us to enjoy together.

- Appreciate the beauty in the world around you.

Holding Hands with My Son

Landon

Some people in this world are huggers. Some are not. My wife's extended family is made up of huggers. This took some getting used to during our first years of marriage when we attended family events. On Krista's father's side of the family there were eleven sets of aunts and uncles. Being of Swiss descent, all felt an embrace was part of a greeting, and many felt the customary cheek kissing should be included. Some regions of Switzerland kiss two or three times on each cheek. When in doubt, three kisses are the goal.

I had been hugged a lot as a young child, especially by my mother, but I wouldn't have described my family as a hugging family. We were 100 percent from Swedish heritage and defaulted, I'm afraid, to the stoic image used to portray Scandinavian people. This emotionally unreactive image may or may not be accurate, however it is safe to say that my wife's Swiss family were more touchy-feely than my extended family of Swedes.

But I married into a family of huggers, so I learned to hug. I did not heartily embrace this act early on, but over the years I have realized something. A hug is a greeting. It is short and sweet. An embrace, however, conveys amazing messages of affirmation and affection.

The result of all this contact was that over time I have become a hugger and perhaps have brought a bit more of it to my own extended family. All my siblings have brought a mix of ideologies to the table with their own relationships with in-laws. I guess we all have contributed a bit more hugging to our family times. Embracing is defined as holding someone closely in one's arms, especially as a sign of affection. This is a good thing...and it gives a sense of belonging. I am glad Solomon felt there was a time to embrace.

An embrace is a statement. It is an acceptance of the other person...one that fully places worth and appreciation in the relationship. It is difficult to embrace someone without sincerely valuing that person, just as they are. We have all felt the demand for the obligatory hug at a wedding or the forced apology and hug we have witnessed as two small children forgive and forget as was suggested by the intervening adults. But an embrace is far more than the physical act of hugging. It is a hug fraught with meaning, emotion, and messages.

Landon, like most young children, was a hugger. I can't exactly place the time when his hugs started turning into embraces, but they did. When Landon hugs someone, there is a message of love and acceptance and value. His embraces can be long and lingering, with no worries about the proper politically-correct length of a hug. This carries over to a lot of Landon's displays of affection and contact with others.

Many times, when Landon and I have been on our adventures together, whether strolling down the aisle of a retail store or taking a walk along a country dirt road, he has reached over to hold my hand. When he was a younger boy, it seemed natural and acceptable to the eyes of any onlookers. Now that he is a man of 23, it tends to feel awkward, at least on my part. I have not grown up in a society that is accustomed to seeing two grown men walking hand in hand. For Landon, it is completely normal. It is an extension of an embrace. It is his way of saying, "Dad...I love you. Thanks for sharing this time with me."

In some foreign countries, men who are friends customarily walk hand in hand. They feel no awkwardness or embarrassment. Like an embrace, it conveys affection and affirmation. Landon gets this. I am still trying to learn.

Due to Landon's periodic weariness, at other times he has laid his head against my shoulder or right down on my lap. When this happens at home while watching a movie, it feels natural to me. However, when we are in a public setting, such as a wedding or a funeral, those feelings of awkwardness start creeping in again. At those times, I always feel the need for people to understand that my grown son has a disability. I want them to know that he doesn't think like most 23-year old men. Then I ask myself, "Why? Why do I feel the need to defend my son's devotion and love?"

That thought brings me back to a time to embrace. I believe that Landon would define embrace in the following way. "An embrace is holding someone closely in one's arms. It is also holding hands or showing other signs of affection to an individual in whom we find immense value." My son is a hugger, an embracer, and an affirmer. He conveys with his actions his love and devotion to those around him. What an amazing lesson of love! Someday I want to learn to embrace my friends as my son does...comfortably and fully from the heart.

- Let the other person end the embrace.

CHAPTER 16:
Growing Independence

As a parent, I have accused myself of holding on too tightly to my children. It is my tendency as a recovering controller. As children reach adolescence and then the teen years it is sometimes difficult to open our hands and begin that process of releasing them into the world. But this is an important steppingstone before letting them spread their wings and launching them.

I have had to do this in diverse ways with each of my children. It was difficult with Joel, our oldest, as I had never done it before. I made many mistakes, and thankfully, he has graciously forgiven me for those years. It is currently difficult with Michaela, who left in January to study abroad in Europe. Right or wrong, it feels different with a daughter. My advice to her comes out somewhat differently than how it did with Joel. With Olivia, who is eighteen and will graduate in a month, I find that I have started the release process a bit earlier with frequent check-in conversations. As parents, it is our job to love, correct, steer, and finally release these God-given blessings. If we have done our job well, they will not only function, but will do well and contribute to our society in a positive way.

With Landon, it has all been so different. As I have already said, due to Landon's years of seizures, there is some effect to his brain similar to a traumatic brain injury. So, my wife and I have had to be sensitive to the desires of his real age, while protecting him at his functional age. This has been a challenge, especially as he has now left his teen years behind.

In his grade-school years, we were always very careful to keep him safe, knowing that a seizure could happen at any moment. We often kept him from childhood activities because of our fear of injury. When we would walk to Grandma's farm, we would throw sticks into the creek underneath "Pooh-Sticks" bridge, as the boys called it.

We always kept one hand on his shirt or arm to keep him from falling in. When we played tag on top of the giant hay bales, which my brother, the farmer, lined up on the back field, one of us was always close by in case he would slip and fall. We often questioned ourselves on being too careful, and yet we felt the need to be good parents.

At a family reunion one summer afternoon, Landon was enjoying himself on a fabulous swing attached high up in the branches of a huge, stately maple tree. In mid-swing, he suddenly flew off and landed with a thud on the ground below. He was having a seizure and had lost consciousness. After it subsided, we carefully checked him and thankfully found no broken bones or injuries. This event only caused us to pull back even harder on our reins and limit his activities to what was deemed "safe" ones, according to us and by our medical team.

Over time and through his teen years, Krista and I began to really question how we were to open our hands and release Landon. He, at times, was so fragile and very much in need of our help. He was unable to even feed himself at the worst of times. He needed one of us to help him while showering and getting dressed. Doling out his cocktail of meds three times a day was something he was unable to do. So, the reality of his growing body desiring more independence proved somewhat more challenging than it did with our other three children.

During the summer of 2015, Landon was hospitalized for 30 days due to cluster seizures that we could not get under control. It was during this time that we, on the urging of our medical team, decided to try the ketogenic diet. This medical diet had helped many children who suffer from seizures gain more seizure control, beyond what medication had been able to do for them. We had tried the diet when Landon was eight years old. It was a horrible nine-month period that did not help curb seizures and only frustrated a young boy with a very restrictive diet. Our apprehension toward trying it once again was obvious, but we were left with few choices regarding new treatments or medications. Throughout the latter part of his hospitalization, we were already seeing positive results from the diet. As we moved back home, the improvements continued. We were seeing some of the best seizure control we had ever experienced. Landon was now almost 20 years old, and it seemed time to start opening those hands again and allowing him a bit more independence.

Landon had been saving money for his own four-wheeler. It was now time to help him purchase one. We had never really thought that he would be able to drive it alone. In fact, it wasn't even a consideration. Up to this point in his life, he was content to drive with one of us riding on the back or riding while one of us was driving. We had often let him ride his bicycle by himself along the road on our back field, but the thought of him operating a motorized vehicle was another thing. Over time, Krista and I came to the same conclusion. We needed to open this door for Landon. It was a great desire of his to drive his four-wheeler by himself.

So began the lessons of how to drive responsibly. Over the next few weeks he amazed us with his growing steadiness on the throttle and his controlled choice of speed. He graduated from driving his instructors around to driving alone with an instructor on the other four-wheeler. After much time, we felt he was ready to take a trip on his own. His solo flight was not to be entered into lightly. However, he was ready to fly, and we could no longer stand in his way. With his daytime seizures almost non-existent during this period, we knew he was on the threshold of that next level of independence. The value of the weeks of lessons were proven by his performance. Not only did he feel total freedom for the first time in his life, but he did an amazing job!

Interestingly, an aspect that goes along with freedom and letting go is the potential for hurt. We unfortunately saw this on his 22nd birthday as Landon had a mishap on his four-wheeler. He ended up with a cast on his foot. For almost two months he was not able to ride his four-wheeler due to a broken ankle and heel. Did he regret his freedom due to this injury? Absolutely not! Did we feel a level of compunction, as parents, because of what had transpired? Surprisingly, no! We realized that increased independence brings with it potential risks. We all live with them, and they are a reasonable trade off when one is desiring an increase in autonomy. Ironically, Krista and I realized that this was the first time Landon had broken a bone due to having fun, rather than due to a seizure!

There is a time to refrain from embracing. Every parent must carefully assess when their child has reached that point in life. It is the time when we slowly but steadily release them to realize their full potential. It is the time when they learn to stand on their own feet and use the wisdom that we, as parents, have infused into them to make good decisions. It is a steppingstone in their independence.

I doubt that Landon will ever drive a car. In fact, his four-wheeler might be as good as it gets for him. But I am thankful that we took the chance and gave him his own opportunity to spread his wings. There are no guarantees in this life. At times, we all must take chances. I know that there is a time to refrain from embracing our children. I am reminded of this every time I see my son drive off on his four-wheeler. I know it in my heart when I see him return with a huge smile on his face, one that can't be duplicated by any other experience on this earth.

- Take chances occasionally.

CHAPTER 17:
Lou

Krista and I met in the fall of 1990. She had been working at a camp near my home, which had been started as a summer camp for children and teens back in the 1950s. Once the vision of a camp was developed, my dad donated his carpentry skills to help build the first cabins. The facility has now turned into a year-round camping and retreat center. Camps are fun. This camp has a great waterfront in the summer and great skiing and inner tubing in the winter. It is an amazing place. It was a special place to meet my wife.

Joel, Michaela, and Olivia attended this camp each summer for a week from elementary through high school years. They loved it, and what kid wouldn't? The food was amazing, the activities were exciting, and the staff was top-notch. Each year they would plan and anticipate attending camp with their friends for a week. Unfortunately, Landon missed out on this. Due to his seizures and medical needs, he could not attend this camp...or any other camp that we knew of...and so we began our time of searching.

The concept of searching was not foreign to us. We had been searching for treatments for his seizures for years. Searching had become a way of life for us. So, we thought finding a camp for a kid with epilepsy couldn't be that difficult.

Around the time Landon was about eleven, we began working with an Epilepsy Foundation in our state. It was 90 miles away, but the woman in charge was caring, witty, and full of energy. She was a real dynamo! Her name was Lou, and she made an immediate connection with Landon. I have a feeling Lou made a connection with every seizure kid she met, but deep down, we told ourselves that Landon was one of her favorites.

Each spring Lou planned an epilepsy walk fundraiser. It was a big event. We got involved with it and began to meet others who also were parenting children who struggled with epilepsy. At one of these walks, we learned about a camp in our state that was established and funded by the Lions Club International. Throughout each summer, it weekly provided five-day camp experiences for visually impaired kids, but it also sponsored a week where kids with epilepsy were invited to join them. When we found out that Lou packed her bags and joined the group each year, we were on board and began to make plans for Landon to attend camp the following summer.

Searching is an interesting thing. Sometimes we search in the wrong places for things, and therefore never find them. Sometimes we search in the right place, but we still cannot find the desired object. Sometimes searching proves no challenge and things are dropped right in our laps, and we wonder how we had never seen it before.

Throughout the next school year, we prepped Landon for his week of camp coming up the following July. His excitement was apparent to all he told about camp. But as the weeks and months rolled by and his week of camp neared, Krista and I began to wonder what we were about to do. We were going to send our special needs son to a place 150 miles away. We were going to leave him there for a week while someone else administered his medications throughout the day, watched him at night for seizures, and cared for him after the seizures occurred...and we were pretty sure the seizures would occur. We began to second guess our decision about camp.

After much encouragement from friends and seeing the excitement mounting in Landon, we knew we had to go forward with the plan. The day we drove him to camp was excruciating emotionally. He had two violent grand mal seizures in the car. At one point, we almost turned around. How could we expect people we had never met to care for our son? But here we were, just ten miles away from the camp. We really felt there was no turning back at that point.

Registration took forever...at least in the health lodge. His health history and med administration were carefully documented as we explained his normal seizures and what he would need during recovery times. They were optimistic and assured us that he would be in good hands with the nurses and Lou on hand. Lou...when she walked through the door, it was like an old friend had come to help us out. We had only met her in person on two occasions...both times at the epilepsy walks. However, Krista had spoken to her many times on the phone. Her presence helped the anxiety subside, at least to a degree.

She walked with us to Landon's cabin as we met his counselor and got him unpacked. And then they expected us to leave...to leave our little boy who couldn't care for himself...our boy who needed us! How could we leave?

But we did say good-bye, and Landon took off with his counselor and cabin buddies. We went to the canteen and enjoyed an hour-long cone with Lou as she talked us off the ledge and assured us that she would be in contact daily letting us know how Landon was doing.

To make a long story short...it was a wonderful week! Oh, he had several seizures. He even had to stay in the health lodge a few nights rather than in his cabin due to the seizures. Not surprising to Krista and me, Landon had every nurse in that lodge wrapped around his little finger.

Landon returned to that camp each summer until he reached the age that he was too old to attend. Some years were better than others, seizure-wise. One year he had to come home early because of the number of seizures, but oh did he love his camp! Every year he returned to Lou and the health lodge workers who loved him and cared for him as if he was their own.

Sometimes when we search, we aren't quite sure what we are searching for or what we will find. When we looked for a camp for Landon, we didn't know what to expect. What we found was a place where he could be a "normal" kid for a week. It was a place where he wasn't "the kid with seizures," but he was simply "one of the kids." We found that not only did he need camp, but so did we. As difficult as it was to trust others to care for our son, it was the right thing to do. It was a week of respite for us, a week to recharge, and a week for Landon to begin his own journey toward a bit of independence away from his family.

We had searched for a camp for Landon, and we had found one. We also found a lifelong friend in Lou. She impacted all of us. In the process, she blessed us far beyond what she could ever know. Her love and encouragement were like pearls found in an oyster shell along the beach. A time to search sometimes brings blessings we would never have imagined!

- Be on the lookout for a new friend in an unusual place.

Turning Corners

I hate to lose! From the days of saying "Uncle" while wrestling with my brothers to playing board games, giving up is not my style. When I start something, I like to see it through. This is my nature in projects and in competition. Throughout my life, I have faced challenging situations. Surrendering has never been an option. My dad taught me to see things through to completion...and in the process to do your best.

My competitive spirit keeps me from giving up. I remember one summer when Krista and I were first married. We were living by a small lake in an A-frame house, preparing for the arrival of our first child. We had an on-going cribbage tournament for several weeks. Now there is an element of luck in cribbage. There is also some solid strategy that needs to be used to be a winner. For weeks on end, we played cribbage. I just could not beat my wife. I was in a losing slump that wouldn't end. One night I was so frustrated with the outcome that I was about to throw the cribbage board into the lake. I opened the sliding door, and then I thought better of the whole idea. Instead, I threw the deck of cards. This shows the emotion, good or bad, that goes into my competitive spirit.

Giving up on puzzles of the mind, such as crosswords and number puzzles, is equally frustrating to me. It simply is not an option. I find logic problems challenging and so satisfying to solve, but admitting defeat is just not a part of it. Consequently, when Solomon says there is a time to give up, I just can't wrap my head around it. Why would we give up?

As a family, our reality has been times of giving up over the years. There are times in this life when, no matter to what level we have pushed or fought to overcome, we must face defeat. We must give up. One of the first of those moments we faced with Landon was giving up on the idea that his seizures would just stop on their own. For the first few months after his initial day of seizures, we had periods, sometimes weeks, where he had none. We chose not to use medication, and we hoped for the best. But six months later when the seizures increased, not only in number but also intensity, we had no choice but to start medication.

I am, and continue to be, a believer in miracles. So, this step of giving up was a difficult one. All these years later I still believe in miracles. I also feel that if God was going to heal Landon, it would have already happened. This has led me to the thought that Landon is who God wants him to be, and perhaps he will touch more lives and bring more good to this world without being healed of his epilepsy.

Another time we have had to give up was through facing reality as Landon grew older. Our dreams for our children have always been to see them grow up healthy, enjoy life, learn from our example and guidance, and find purpose and meaning in their adult lives as God leads them. We have dreamed that they would find someone to love and share their life with, a career that brings enjoyment, and perhaps grandchildren for us someday. Many of these dreams for Landon we have had to abandon, at least for now. The reality of his life and his seizures was not paving the way to those dreams.

It was difficult and painful, and it has taken most of Landon's lifetime for me to face this step of giving up. But in the last few years, we have seen doors open to him. In his current employment, he is finding happiness, fulfillment, and purpose... beyond what our shattered dreams could have imagined. In our process of "giving up," we have found new hopes and dreams. They are different from the ones we anticipated. We are now witnessing the pursuance and even the completion of some of them.

There is a time to give up. I am learning this lesson slowly. It is no longer so difficult to give up, for I am finding that when we give up, we turn a corner. We don't hit a dead end. There is another choice, another option, another reality around that corner. Without the conscious effort of giving up, we would never find that new reality. Each of those acts of giving up leads us to the next step in this life...and one step closer to finding God's purpose for our existence on this earth. Landon is finding purpose in life and fulfillment in what he does. This has brought him happiness, even though he still struggles with seizures. God has a plan for Landon...a good plan to prosper him. Without learning to give up, we would never have been able to help him pursue that plan.

- Begin the process of releasing something that has caused you emotional pain.

Our country is full of treasures. Some are historical like the Declaration of Independence. It cannot be replaced. Some are natural like the Badlands of South Dakota. They cannot be taken in with one viewing. Some are personal like my grandmother's crystal cream and sugar bowl given to my wife by my mother. It is one-of-a-kind. Treasures have stories.

Several years ago, I bought a metal detector. I just knew I was going to find some amazing treasures that would make me a rich man. I used that detector on beaches, in open fields, and on well-traveled walking paths through the woods. I found soda cans, bottle tops, paper clips, a few coins, and one very dull knife on the shore of Lake Michigan. None of those things made me wealthy, but I have still enjoyed using my metal detector. I find excitement in the prospect of finding an amazing treasure on my next outing.

I have some antiques in my house. At one time, I enjoyed going to auctions and bidding on these old treasures. I have acquired many over the years, sometimes having spent more than I should. Some of these items truly are treasures, but most of them have lost their attraction over time. They have no connection to my life...no story interwoven with me. Without the connection, they eventually become less and less valuable. Aside from dishes and heirlooms passed on to me from my parents, I have only a few antiques that I truly value.

One of these is an old stand up Edison victrola. It came with 50 records...the old kind that could double as second base. Even though the victrola had no story for me and no connection to my family, it has become valuable over time. My children grew up asking to listen to it, and we enjoyed many hours winding it up and hearing its old melodies.

We changed records every five minutes and danced together around the living room. I remember one special night when my Uncle Reuben and Aunt Doris, who grew up during The Great Depression, sat visiting with us in our living room. For a few hours they reminisced about old times as we listened to the victrola.

Another antique I still appreciate is an old church pew that my dad purchased for me from an auction. He knew that I liked antiques and bid on it in my absence. The fact that my dad thought of me and my hobby of antiquing brings this old pew its value. The connection I have with it came long after weekly parishioners sat uncomfortably on its darkened wood. Once I got it to my house and my dad realized it was too long, he cut it in half and rebuilt it, much shorter than the original, to become a usable bench in my house. It continues to remind me of my connection with my dad and my love for him.

Yet another antique that I would have difficulty parting with is an old rocking chair with a "Man in the Wind" face on the back. I have no idea who owned it before or any of its stories, except for the ones my family made with it. My wife and I rocked each of our four children in that old chair, right from the time we brought them home from the hospital. It is filled with love and nostalgia. It is a rare treasure.

The final antique that I truly see as a treasure is an old pump organ. I bought it before I was married, and it sat in a crowded corner of my bedroom during my first few years of teaching while I was still living in my parents' house. It played well right from the time I bought it, and my mom loved it. It reminded her of the years she played the pump organ in many churches as a young girl.

When I first bought the organ, I took the front panel off to inspect it. I found the original manufacturer's slip dated 1869. I used to tell my children how this very organ was made only four years after President Lincoln was killed. Every Christmas Eve they begged me to play it and I happily obliged them with Christmas carols. The organ has gained value as we have added our own stories and memories.

All of that brings me to Landon and the treasure hanging in his bedroom. I have no idea what its value is monetarily, but it has a story and a connection to his life and is therefore a true treasure. Treasures are defined as valuable objects, but often the value is in sentiment and memories rather than money.

Randall Cunningham was a famous NFL quarterback. He played in the NFL for 16 seasons, most of them with the Philadelphia Eagles. Randall, himself, struggled with childhood seizures. After his tenure in the NFL, Randall Cunningham chose a different career path. He became an evangelist and eventually an ordained minister in his quest to serve God. He currently pastors a church in Las Vegas, Nevada.

During the time that we were praying for Lynnette as a family, a woman in our church told her brother about Landon. He happened to live in Las Vegas and attended Randall's church. One day he was meeting with his pastor for coffee. He told him about this little boy, Landon, and how his uncontrolled seizures were negatively affecting his life. Randall immediately got up, walked into the next room, and came back with an official Philadelphia Eagles jersey, Number 12. He took out a pen and autographed it. Handing it to the young man he said, "You get this jersey to that little boy."

The jersey was presented to Landon by the woman from our church on Super Bowl Sunday, 2006, in front of our entire congregation. This was just two months after our disheartening return from Cleveland. When they put it on him, it looked like a dress. At the time Landon didn't understand the significance of a sports hero giving him such a valuable gift. He did understand that somebody famous, who loved Jesus and also had suffered from uncontrollable seizures during his childhood, chose to give him something special and make a connection with him.

Landon's Grandpa Henry built a large display case to house the jersey, and this has hung in his room ever since. For the first several years, Landon brought any guest in our house down to his room to see his jersey...his treasure. One cannot enter his room and ignore the grand presence of this huge jersey and display case on the wall.

Treasures without a story eventually lose their charm, regardless of their monetary worth. Therein lies their real worth. Solomon was rich, and he liked his treasures. If he could visit our home, I would have a few things to show him. After hearing their stories, I believe he would encourage us to keep them...especially the jersey!

- Tell someone the story behind one of your treasures.

CHAPTER 20:
Decluttering and Persevering

I have recently been on a cleaning spree in our house. Last summer, since I had decided not to teach summer school, I thought it was time to do a thorough cleaning and decluttering of every room. This is easier said than done, for I have concluded that I am somewhat of a hoarder.

I know some people who throw away too much. If they haven't used it this month, if they haven't worn it recently, if they don't like it anymore, it's gone! I have seen people spend hundreds of dollars on things like exercise equipment only to let it sit and then get rid of it a few months later. I have seen brand new clothing with the tags still attached dropped off at a resale shop. This doesn't make sense to me, but as I admitted, I am a saver.

I know others who can't seem to throw anything away. A few years ago, I talked to a friend who was helping her neighbor pack up her home for a cross-country move. This lady had 22 complete sets of dishes and china...22! Her garage was an organized garage-sale paradise. I strive to be somewhere between these two extremes.

So, as I began this cleaning and decluttering assignment, I found myself constantly laboring over the decision of whether to keep or to throw. Over the years, my wife and I, mostly at my urging, have saved plastic tubs of school papers, baby clothes, toys, and other memories for each of our children. We have a few closets devoted totally to the storage of items we don't currently use and never will. It is stuff!

I read a book several years ago when I began this venture to reform from saving too much. The premise was to touch each questionable item in your home. If it didn't give you a warm feeling due to its usefulness or special memories then out it went. I must confess there have been times when I told my wife we could get rid of some things, and I have slyly hauled them to my storage area at school, just in case I might need them later. A recent television show encourages people who struggle with throwing away to haul everything out of a particular room and make three piles outside. One pile is to save, one pile is to throw, and one is to sell or give away. I've wondered how many of those people haul most of those items right back into their house.

Throwing away is difficult for me. I like the feel of things in my hands that can evoke memories. But the reality is the memories will still be there, even when the clutter is gone. Landon is good at this. He keeps things for a while, often things I cannot understand why he would want them. He keeps sticks, empty shell casings from a rifle, pieces of paper, old crayons, and miscellaneous junk. (Why is it that my stuff is good stuff while other people's stuff is junk?)

When the time comes to clean out and organize his room Landon freely gives up those things that are no longer important to him. He doesn't labor over the decision. He just says, "Throw it!" He knows the memories will still be there, minus the rubble. Incidentally, decluttering his bedroom was so much easier than dealing with mine.

In the book of Hebrews, we are told to "throw off everything that hinders and the sin that so easily entangles." (Hebrews 12:1a; NIV) This doesn't just mean to only throw away the junk in our houses, but also the junk in our lives. Some of this junk we've been saving for years, perhaps even hoarding. Just as easily as Landon can throw away stuff that has become tangible junk to him, he can also throw those things that hinder him. He consistently throws away resentment, bad attitudes, and negativity. Imagine the world we would live in if everyone threw away that junk in their lives. This is the world in which Landon lives. He sees the good and believes the best because his mind is focused on the best. He has cleared out the clutter.

Hebrews goes on to encourage us to "...run with perseverance the race marked out for us." (Hebrews 12:1b; NIV) Runners know this. To successfully run a race, they must throw off the things that encumber them. That is how they persevere, stay the course, and finish the race.

I still have things to throw away in my house. I always will. Someday my children will go through my possessions after I am gone from this earth, and they will wonder why their dad saved all this junk! Call it stuff, things, or possessions...it's all still junk!

As for my life, I also have some junk, some scrap, some rubble to throw away. That is the junk that concerns me more. I spend far too much time being encumbered with negative stuff. That is another benefit of spending time with Landon. Daily, he demonstrates for me how to throw away the refuse in our lives...the garbage in this world. He is a picture of perseverance and positivity, and that is the key to finishing the race of life strong and uncluttered.

- Get rid of something that is holding you back.

CHAPTER 21

Creating and Contentment

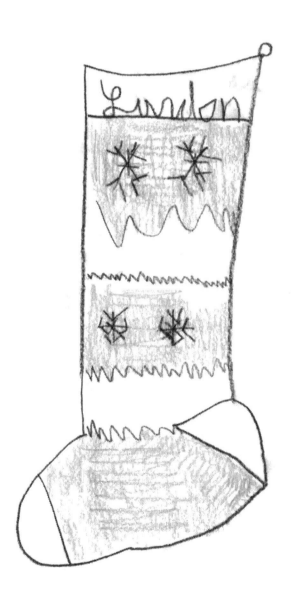

My mother was an amazing seamstress. As a young woman, she sewed many of her own clothes during The Great Depression. She would remake clothes from what had been given to her. Years later when she had her own seven children, she sewed many outfits for each one. When my oldest sister got married, she sewed not only her wedding dress, but also three bridesmaid dresses and several suit coats for my brothers and me.

Not only could she sew, but she was also an accomplished quilter. Each of the six bedrooms in our old farmhouse had a colorful quilt gracing the bed. These were made over time from scraps of material, old clothing, and yard goods she purchased. The result was a work of art. When I left for college, she made a new quilt for me. I used it through my four years of schooling. When I got married and started my own household it followed me there. Now over 35 years later, it has gotten tattered in some places, but it is special nonetheless and, you guessed it...I won't part with it!

My mom also could knit faster than anyone I know. Her hands and fingers moved like a machine when she was knitting. She made beautiful sweaters and vests for all her children. One of these I wore all through college and even afterward. Eventually the weight I had gained during those early married years forced me to stop wearing it. She made us wool socks every winter that were warmer than any store-bought socks. By the time my children came along she made them special slipper socks to wear around the house on chilly winter nights.

In her later years, she loved to crochet. Her creations were envied by many. My daughters received dresses for their dolls with matching hats and scarves for themselves. Each of her grandchildren received a beautiful quilt upon their high school graduation.

These she would make while watching football on television. All these acts of creating became second nature to my mom. She was a true master of these arts.

Part of sewing, quilting, knitting, and crocheting is the unfortunate task of tearing or ripping. This is a necessary process when mistakes are made, and work needs to be redone. My mom always got a bit frustrated when she had to do this. Not only did it create more work. It was a reminder that we make mistakes and we need to fix them. Sometimes this happens when we aren't focused. Distractions in this life tend to make us tear and redo more than we want.

One holiday my mom knit Christmas stockings for each of her children, their spouses, the grandchildren and their spouses, and the great-grandchildren. 51 stockings in all were created! Each one was about 22 inches long, lined with satin, and knitted into it was a picture of a winter or holiday scene. Each one also included the name of the person. We were all amazed at her workmanship, as well as the time she had put into these special gifts.

In the years following that Christmas, she would make stockings for any new great-grandchildren that had joined us during the previous year. But as she neared the end of her life knitting became more and more difficult. She often had to do more tearing, sometimes entire sections. Mom grew more aggravated with herself that her mind had seemingly forgotten the skill and her fingers were not working as adeptly as they once had. The letters in the names were often uneven. The tearing part of the production was now becoming more of the process than it ever had before.

Life is a lot like that. We work, we progress, and then we tear. It's not fun, and it is often painful. We never seem to get beyond the point of making mistakes. They are a part of our lives, and tearing is a part of fixing them, regardless of what we expect of ourselves.

Last week when I picked up Landon from work, I was surprised to find him in a different section of the complex. When we got in the van, I asked him how his day was. He responded, "Just great!" I asked what he had been doing way in back. He told me, "I got to shred today!" Shredding! He was shredding paper, and he was loving it! Shredding is kind of like tearing. It is taking something apart. Landon was fully enjoying his work of tearing, and it gave me a new thought. What if we looked at our tearing in life as not only necessary, but truly embraced it as a part of the process and found enjoyment in it.

As he fell asleep on the way home, my mind wandered to another thought. God is the only Creator who doesn't need to tear. His creation is exactly right. In the book of Psalms, the writer says, "You knit me together in my mother's womb..." (Psalm 139:13b; NIV) Many people have asked me over the years why Landon has seizures. They ask what is wrong with his body that causes them. I could give them the medical diagnosis, but over time I have realized that there is nothing wrong with my son. He is the creation that God intended. Although parts of his body have caused struggles and pain, his life is one of purpose and worth. I would be tempted, due to my humanity, to "tear apart" and remake or fix the parts of Landon that cause his seizures. Many view my son as imperfect and broken...needing repair...but don't all of us have scars and cracks, tears and imperfections?

God knew when He knit Landon together that seizures would be a part of him. He knew that those seizures would not beat him. He knew that Landon would rise above them and live a life of contentment and purpose amidst the struggles. Landon's faith and resilience cause him to overcome the seizures and their effects in a way that has helped others see his love for life. They have seen his faith in action. In that, there are no mistakes. No tearing is needed.

There is a time to tear. It is not always when or what we think needs tearing. Though it may cause pain in our lives, it is a step to becoming who we are meant to be. We all need to do a little tearing at times. If we can maintain a sense of acceptance, the process of fixing will help us to mature as people. It will also bring us to a place of contentment in life. Of all the lessons I have learned from my son, one of the greatest of these is to live the life I have been given with contentment. It is how Landon lives each day of his life.

- Seek true contentment in the life you have been given.

CHAPTER 22:
Fixing and Forgiving

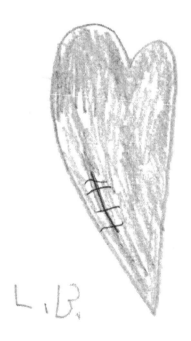

Things in this life need mending. To mend means to repair something that is broken or damaged. Mending can take a lot of work and it often requires an expert to do the job properly. Things in this world wear out, break, or get damaged. Consequently, there is a need for people to mend. When mending is needed, some people find it easier to just throw things out. Mending takes skill and patience. When mending is done properly those broken and damaged items can be used again.

I have seen many things mended in my lifetime. My mother mended many articles of clothing in our youth. Money was tight, and her skill with a needle and thread saved thousands of dollars that new clothes would have cost. I don't think a day went by on our farm that one of us boys didn't rip out the crotch or the knees in a pair of jeans. My mom not only mended them, but she also inserted patches that lasted and looked good, too. I remember people commenting that "...nobody could patch a pair of pants like Mabel could."

Growing up on the farm, I also helped mend a lot of fences. When done well our cows stayed in the field where they belonged. When we carelessly or hurriedly mended fences, we often got phone calls from our neighbors. I remember chasing cows in the middle of the night on several occasions. Sometimes they were on the road, down by the lake, or even in the woods. Farmers know that good fences are necessary. Without good fences cows get out, and neighbors get ruffled. I learned to use a mall and a hammer, and I learned to stretch the wire tightly until the next time a wayward bovine chose to wander.

Sometimes reputations need mending. First impressions can often taint an otherwise good reputation. Bad decisions can also damage what others think of us. Reputations are a bit harder to mend than clothing or fences. Rather than tools like needle and thread or hammer and mall, we need time, effort, and good choices. Sadly, some people never recover from these situations and the mending process becomes almost impossible.

I have had to mend a few friendships over the years. Judgmental or angry words spoken in haste have damaged relationships, sometimes seemingly beyond repair. Again, this mending process takes time, humility, and a sincere decision to begin the process of rebuilding. At times in my life, I have been on both sides of a friendship that needed mending. It is always painful.

Often, my life has needed mending. I have messed up and hurt others. I have hurt myself. I have acted too quickly. I have misjudged. These are attitudes and actions that humble me, but when I can effectively mend these things, I begin the process of healing. I admire people who don't need as much mending as I do. I'm not sure if this is because they make smaller mistakes or better choices. I know they spare themselves the emotional anguish that accompanies mending.

Landon has taught me two lessons in this area. First, because he believes the best in others and rarely judges them, he doesn't have to do a lot of mending. On those occasions when he speaks or acts before he thinks or is disrespectful to someone, usually one of his siblings, he tries to make it right. When one is careful, mending becomes the exception rather than the norm. A second thing I have seen in my son is when others need to mend. When they have hurt, misjudged, or treated him harshly he immediately has an attitude of forgiveness in his heart. It's not for show. It's not a charade. It is a true forgiveness with a desire for restoration.

When he was a small child, we taught Landon that this is how God forgives us. In his child-like faith he learned this. As a young man who has been able to securely maintain this same child-like faith, perhaps partly due to his disability, he follows the example of His Heavenly Father. Forgiveness is sincere, quick, and complete. It allows him to segue on to the next journey in life, unencumbered by resentment. Landon's response to mending reminds me that grudges make us bitter; but forgiveness sets us free.

Mending broken or damaged relationships is a part of life, but it allows us to heal and bring newness to something others might just toss. A time to mend often takes humility, but it is a part of fixing in this life. It's a part of the true forgiveness that I see in Landon's heart…the forgiveness he learned from his Heavenly Father…the forgiveness that can change this world.

- Allow yourself to forgive someone who has hurt you.

Over the years our busy household revolved around homework, jobs, and sports schedules. Whenever we found ourselves home together, there was usually noise...lots of noise! When six people live together, silent moments are usually relegated to nighttime and sleeping. Mealtimes at our house have always been filled with stories and laughter as we recollected our days. Sometimes there was even noise generated through arguments, believe it or not. Suffice it to say we have grown accustomed to noise over the years in our family.

Before my wife worked outside of the home, she would occasionally take the kids to her parents' house an hour away for overnight stays during the summer months. This usually happened on hot, muggy days, and her parents' pool was a definite draw. Of course, the kids loved to visit Grandpa and Grandma, as well. Because I was usually teaching summer school, I would often stay behind. On those warm and sticky evenings, I would experience true silence. I didn't need to use my voice. I would sit on the deck with a good book and enjoy the peacefulness only interrupted by birds, wind chimes, and an occasional breeze through the trees.

I think everyone needs times of silence. Our lives become so filled up with commitments and expectations that we rarely sit down and just enjoy noiseless moments of tranquility. Our busy lives need a break at times, not just from activity, but also from noise. These are the moments that bring healing and reprieve. These moments are cathartic. Like a balm, they bring comfort to our weariness from the pressing obligations of life.

Landon has had many periods in his life where he was silent. Recovering from a night of seizures is exhausting, especially when the night spreads into months of nights. That recovery time was often filled with silence.

In Landon's times of silence, he has learned to be a great listener. This is another skill lacking in our world today. I admire this trait in my son. Many of us converse with others, not attentively listening, but just waiting for our chance to say what we want. As soon as the other person pauses to draw a breath, we let loose with an explosion of words. Silence helps us practice the skill of listening. It helps us listen to people, to nature, or even just listen to silence itself.

Landon truly enjoys the art of listening. He becomes fully engulfed in the conversations and the stories of others. He commits these tales to memory. He can often remember stories that I have shared verbatim, and he is quick to remind me of each detail that I leave out with the next telling. Silence goes hand in hand with listening. I have found that my son is not afraid of silence. His amazing memory is due, in part, to a commitment to listen silently to those around him who are talking. What a gift!

Some people in this world are afraid of silence. In my college teaching courses, we were told by our professors that silence in a classroom while waiting for an answer is not a bad thing. When a teacher asks a question, they should allow time for the question to be heard, processed, and for a response to be formulated. Many students need this time. The temptation is to get rid of that "awkward silence" and elicit an answer as quickly as possible.

Our world is full of sound. Many people presume to find comfort in surrounding themselves with it. We freely add it to our days and call it background noise. We rarely spend an evening in our homes without the addition of it from electronic sources.

Our world is also full of silence, and I believe it can have a greater, more comforting effect upon us if we only allow ourself to experience it. Silence brings with it the opportunity to reflect, to relax, and to heal.

In some of the darkest periods of Landon's seizure activity, he has actually been unable to speak. At times, we went for days without hearing his voice. This was not a chosen silence on his part, but one that was quite out of our control.

During one of these times, when he was about six years old, Landon and I began a system of communication. After a seizure, I would ask him a question and put my index finger inside his fist. He would squeeze my finger to communicate with me. Not only did this system allow him to answer "yes" or "no" to my questions, but it soon developed into a silent way to share his feelings. In better times, even when he was able to speak, he would quietly reach over, grab my finger, and squeeze it. I asked him one day what that meant, and he responded, "It means I love you, Dad."

Some of the most important things in this world require no voice. Some of our deepest and most meaningful emotions can be conveyed in silence. It can draw us closer to nature and to others. It even allows us to hear what has always been there, but we've missed it due to the excessive noise in our lives. My son knows how to be silent. He has even learned how to use those moments to express his deep love to others. He has shown me that when we are silent, we often can speak more clearly from our hearts.

- Learn to appreciate the silent moments of life.

Landon

Verbal communication is at the heart of relationships. It enables us to affirm, support, and bring deeper meaning to our connections with others. It, unfortunately, can also be used to destroy. It is a very powerful entity. It is estimated that there are over seven thousand languages in the world today. Just as silence is important in our lives, there is an equally valuable time to speak. Communication with those in our lives has the power to be both nurturing and formidable.

I speak a lot in my line of work. Some would say I make my living with my mouth. All that talking has the potential to produce daily faux pas in the delivery. My first-grade students love when I get to talking too fast and strange things come out of my mouth. There are days when I get home from school, and I just don't have many words left in me. Those are the evenings that I quietly read or watch a movie. I once read that an average woman uses over 20,000 words each day and the average man uses only 7,000. Even if my quota is well above the average man, this statistic, if true, tells me that I am well over my allocation of words by the end of most school days.

Landon's first spoken word was "tukka tukka" (tickle tickle). This was soon followed by "Dada." After those first words were uttered, the rest came fast and furious. Even at an early age, he loved to talk and tell stories. His tales were always full of vivid description and big words. They were accompanied by an energetic voice and sparkling eyes. People often commented on Landon's vocabulary. When he heard a new, big word he would try to use it in conversation. Often, he used it incorrectly. Even when he didn't, it was humorous hearing a preschooler conjure up adult-sized words and fit them into his conversations.

There is power in the spoken word. Jesus calmed a storm with just a word. He also healed sick people with just a few words. The spoken word brings meaning to our lives. As a writer there are times when I labor over just the right word to use. Even during the writing of this book, there have been times when I have changed a word, only to labor over the replacement, and then to change it back at a later reading.

I love the words Landon chooses. He pictures in his mind what he wants to communicate. Then he picks the perfect word to bring meaning to his audience. To this day, he continues to be a storyteller like he was in his earlier years before his seizures started.

Recently we experienced one of those moments when I picked him up from work. I asked my normal question, "How was your day, Buddy?" He looked at me and declared, "It was sparkly!"

When I asked him what that meant, he responded, "A sparkly day is one of those days where everything is great. Nothing bad happened and when you get to the end of it you just know it was sparkly!" Then he asked me if I ever have sparkly days at work. I pondered this as I drove down the highway. To be honest, I don't usually describe my work days as sparkly, regardless of how good they have been.

I was a few minutes late picking him up from work a few weeks later. The buses taking the other employees had already left. I asked him if he was worried, and he said to me, "Dad...I try not to get worried about things in life. I knew you were coming." His response caused me to consider how many more sparkly days I would have if I chose not to worry so much about things or details.

There are over 200,000 words in the English language. Over 40,000 of these words are presently considered obsolete. Landon and I both want to see more words become obsolete. Words that hurt others and keep us from truly enjoying life; negative words that bring us down and cause us to forget how truly blessed we are; these are words that we don't want to allow in our language. These are words we don't want to use to describe our days.

If I could make it a practice to see more of my days as "sparkly" days, I believe I could bring more of that sparkliness to those with whom I work and to those in my own home. If I could add a bit more sparkle to the times I speak, just think what a difference it could make. I know Landon does this. He speaks, he adds sparkle to this world, and in doing so, I believe he makes a difference in the lives of others, even when a time to speak is encompassed in just one solitary word!

- Describe the sparkly parts of your day to someone and add some sparkle to theirs.

CHAPTER 25:
Landon's Definition of Love

L.B

I am prone to believe that almost every book in the world has an angle of love within its pages. If love isn't obviously evident, we might find hate, revenge, loneliness, or any other number of human emotions that stem from love or the lack of it. This book is about love. I have woven the theme into each page. Love as a noun is an intense feeling of deep affection. As a verb love takes on a much higher level of meaning. But can we really put love into a trite definition and have the emotion truly be encompassed?

The Greek society believed that there were six levels of love. Eros was a passionate love, often seen as irrational, fiery, and dangerous. Philia was a love of deep friendship or brotherhood, embodied by loyalty and sacrificial love. Ludus was a playful love, often seen in young children or in adolescent or teenage flirting. Agape was selfless and unconditional love, and it is seen today as the highest level of love in Christian circles. Pragma was the love of long-standing relationships such as "old married couples." It leaned on patience and tolerance learned over time. Finally, philautia was self-love, which the Greeks felt could become unhealthy if one became too self-obsessed. Enough for the Greek lesson on love.

Since I only know a few Greek people, I asked Landon one day what he thought love was. He said, "...when you actually, truly care for someone for always." I have, for years, observed the way Landon loves. He does so deeply from a gracious heart. When one loves in this way, the impact they have on others cannot be measured. It makes me smile when I see the capacity of love in Landon's heart.

I don't know how many types of love Landon will experience in his lifetime. I'm also not sure if our lives are more accurately measured by how much we love or how much we are loved by others. What I do know is how I feel when Landon tells me, "I love you." Sometimes he does this with words. At other times, when words are an exhausting effort due to seizures, he shows me the "I love you" sign from American Sign Language. I also know how very thankful I am that my special needs son has the capacity to express his love to me and to others.

In our time at the Cleveland Clinic several years ago, Krista and I met many families who were facing critical surgeries much more serious than our own. Many of these people were from other countries, some separated from their other children and their spouses to spend months seeking answers and cures. Many of these children were unable to speak. Some of them had never spoken. I am sure that many of them had their own way of communicating "I love you" to their parents. Not a day goes by that I take for granted Landon's ability to convey his love to me and his ability to speak the words.

The power of love is unbelievable! It paves the way for forgiveness and understanding. It changes lives. Its effects are long and far-reaching in this world. The Apostle Paul wrote his famous words about love to the Corinthian church. Here is what he had to say:
    "Love is patient, love is kind. It does not envy, it does not boast, it is not proud. It does not dishonor others, it is not self-seeking, it is not easily angered, it keeps no record of wrongs. Love does not delight in evil but rejoices with the truth. It always protects, always trusts, always hopes, always perseveres." (I Corinthians 13:4-7)

I began this chapter surmising that most books have been written with some connection to love. I doubt that any author can truly understand every aspect of love. I am amazed at how much my son seems to grasp about the topic. As I read Paul's description of love from Corinthians, I see many parallels to Landon's life.

In the midst of living with special needs he has found the ability to truly love. Perhaps his challenges in life have even aided the quest to love sincerely from the heart.

Characteristically, he is patient. I have seen many sacrificial acts of kindness in his dealings with others. He is not envious of others but accepts his situation. He doesn't boast. He is not prideful. Dishonoring others is the exception and he is not self-seeking. He doesn't easily get angry and quickly forgets those acts where he has been wronged. He doesn't delight in evil, but cheers for the truth. He does his best to protect, trust, hope, and persevere. I am deeply humbled that I, who in the world's eyes do not have a disability, struggle with many of these character traits that accompany love. Because of the baggage I carry I often crowd out some of these characteristics. Baggage of the heart is a disability in its own way.

I believe God smiles when He sees the capacity of love within Landon's heart. I believe God has placed that ability to love within Landon's very soul. Landon loves people. He also loves many other things and has helped me to more fully appreciate them…things like snow, falling leaves, sunsets, family times, birds singing, the sound of water, bedtime stories, memories, bicycle rides, winks, flashlights, swinging, and storytelling.

In Landon's eyes TO LIVE IS TO LOVE. When I walk in his shoes and when I make the effort to see things through his eyes, I see love throughout this world in some very unique places. Besides the Bible, if I were to read another authoritative book about love, I believe I would choose one authored by Landon. He seems to know a lot about the topic. I am so thankful God has enabled my son to see every single day as a time to love.

- Love deeply without reservation.

CHAPTER 26:
What Landon Hates

Seizures

L.B

Hate is a strong word. It conveys a complete dislike of something. When our children were younger, we tried to avoid the word hate, and we tried to discourage them from using it. They absolutely were not allowed to use the word in relation to how they felt about another person.

I have some friends that hate certain foods. Eggplant, liver, onions, radishes, and oysters are all on the list. Although I have tried them several times, I must admit I am not a fan of Brussels sprouts. In fact, I hate them! But a hatred of foods is not usually a serious issue. One simply avoids those foods. This only poses a problem when one is meeting their prospective in-laws and the entree is oyster and eggplant pate'.

I know several people who hate shopping. I am one of them. Even though I thoroughly enjoy giving gifts to others, the act of searching for that elusive gift is often tiresome, stressful, and hated! I have learned to shop online when the need arises. I have stretched myself and can manage an afternoon of shopping when it involves spending time with my daughters, however the focus is on togetherness and not on the shopping. It takes all of my acting ability to appear that I am not dying a slow death in a mall, but the time with them brings worth, purpose, and new perspective to an otherwise hated activity.

People from Wisconsin often complain about the seasons. They say that they hate summer because it is too hot and humid. They say that they hate winter because it is too cold and lasts too long! They hate spring because it is wet and muddy, and they even hate fall because, of all things, it is too short!

A lot of Americans hate work. They find themselves in jobs and careers they do not like. They live only for the weekends. Others like their work, but they hate the conflict they face daily at their job. Ideal work situations are hard to come by. There is always that irksome co-worker, the supervisor who doesn't understand, or the long hours. But we need money to live, so many of us go right on hating our work and doing nothing about it.

The list goes on and on. People hate things. They hate poverty, social injustice, law enforcement issues, prejudice, and animals. Some even hate getting older. However, when given the alternative they often see things differently.

Others claim that they hate certain people. Some of these are people who have hurt them, people from past relationships, or perhaps even unknown people whom they fear. Some hate people from history who have done infamous wrongs to humankind. Some hate politicians who are arrogant or professional athletes who are cocky.

The point is we all use the word, the "h" word, at various times in our lives. I personally hate snakes. I hate divorce when it hurts children. I hate cancer. I hate unresolved conflicts. I also hate bananas. There is a lot of hatred in this world, and it exists at varying degrees of intensity. Solomon said that there is a time to hate, but I don't think he ever foresaw the extent to which people would be hating and acting upon that feeling.

The Bible speaks of God hating sin. I personally think that makes sense. Sin is the base for all the evil and hurt in this world. Eliminating sin would solve all our problems. It is a good thing to hate.

In all his 23 years I have only heard Landon declare his hatred for ONE thing. Landon hates seizures. He doesn't dwell on this feeling. In fact, it's only on rare occasions that I actually hear him say it. But he does hate seizures. Truly, they are hateful!

His hatred of them seems completely justified and logical to me. If I could walk in my son's shoes, I believe I would add to his list of things to be hated. These things would be excessive medications, the side-effects from them, hospitalizations, lack of answers, and finally, being misunderstood by others due to a disability.

Many people in our society overuse the concept of hatred in their words and as they relate to what really are intrusions or inconveniences of their lives. I, too, am guilty of trivializing such a strong word. Landon, however, reserves the word for just one thing. Because of this fact, it makes his hatred seem more valid in my mind. I agree with Landon. I hate seizures, too. My hatred of them has grown over the past 19 years due to their unfair assault on my son. I find that they perfectly embody a time to hate.

- Identify something hurtful that is hated and do your best to eradicate it.

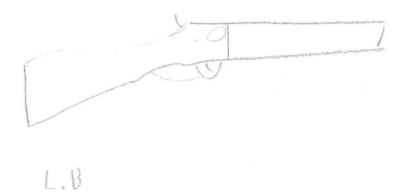

L.B

I had several majors of study in college before I finally settled on Elementary Education. It took two years to decide, but once I made the decision, I knew that it was a perfect fit! I knew I was meant to be in the classroom. But if I had chosen to teach at the high school or college level, I would have taught History. I love to read history and I love to learn about history. History intrigues me!

A large part of world and American history deals with wars. I have read about most of them, whether in the historical fiction or nonfiction genres. I have found that wars involve people of diverse ethnicities and classes, but the underlying theme is always the same. There is a quest for power, a misunderstanding, and lack of respect for the passions and beliefs of others.

My oldest son, Joel, is currently in graduate school. I try to check in with him several times a week. Occasionally he messages me after his exams. Recently, in the midst of a finals week lasting seven days, including thirteen exams he said, "Dad...that one was a real killer!" I reminded him that it was just one battle, and not the war!

Several years ago, Krista and I participated in a parenting class with some friends. One of the prevailing themes I came away with was, "Choose carefully the hill you're willing to die on." In other words, not every issue in parenting is worth the battle. Making every issue a battle is never productive and tears down the relationship with your child. I have attempted to choose those "hills" carefully in my parenting. When I have been successful, it has proven to be good advice.

We also use the war and battle metaphors in many areas of our society. Think of the wars in our country that have little or nothing to do with weapons. We have the war on poverty, the war on drugs, the war on terror, the war on crime, the war on cancer, and even the war on car emissions. The metaphor is a useful one since we all have a basic understanding about war, or at least a fear of it. The threat of war stirs our emotions and incites us to battle against unjust societal issues that affect our lives.

Through my study of World War II, I have read stories of the patriotism and passion on the home front in our country. As soldiers went off to war in distant lands, those at home did what they could to help the effort. Scrap metal drives, rubber drives, and rationing were things all Americans were expected to do. Children and adults became a part of the war effort at home. The unity exhibited in our country has not since been surpassed. Churches, schools, and entire communities supported families whose fathers and brothers were away at war. I had five uncles fighting in various theaters of the war. Two of them were wounded in action. Unity was very important to my grandparents and to the entire American populace during that time.

My immediate family has been fortunate. The only war we have fought in is the war against seizures. Though devastating in its own way, it is a figurative war. We have battled seizures and the misunderstandings of my son for years. It has been a long and hard-fought conflict. We have formed battle plans seeking favorable outcomes. We have joined efforts to legislate new forms of available treatment. We have fought valiantly and been emotionally worn down at times. I have been the general periodically, and at other times it has been my wife. We have fought hard to defend one of our own soldiers, Landon. But even when I consider the passion we have expended in our fight; I cannot compare it to those families who have been torn apart and have buried family members in literal wars. War evokes strong emotions and a call for action at its mention. It is a fierce and powerful word. Anyone who has endured a war, especially in their own land, does not walk away unscathed. Wars are destructive and horrific. Unfortunately, they are a reality of our world. Solomon said that there is a time for war, so we know they were also a reality of the ancient world.

I have never been a soldier. I pray the same for my children, unless they feel led to do so. Most of us cannot understand what it means to devote ourselves to a cause that demands the ultimate sacrifice. The gratitude I feel to those men and women, past and present, cannot adequately be expressed with mere words.

Each of us has battled in our own ways. Throughout our lives we are called to fight unique private wars. These are the dark wars in our hearts and minds that we try to keep hidden from others. These, too, require a battle plan to ultimately seek a favorable outcome.

We, as a family, have fought our war against seizures in this way. We have been unable to emerge unaffected at the other end of each battle. Seizures have taken a toll, but along the way we have been able to unify ourselves with others. Sometimes we have carried each other, but mostly others have carried us. Their support has been the hand of God in our lives, and their solidarity with us has helped us grow in our faith.

Unity has been a part of every successful battle plan through the years. It is the bond that holds us together and brings us strength during conflict. That unity has joined us with others, in our war against seizures, to provide support, trust, and belief. Like those American citizens, supporting the brave soldiers of WWII, I choose unity; and it is a "hill" on which I am willing to die.

- Seek and strive for unity in hard times.

CHAPTER 28:
Home

In the Book of Romans in the New Testament of the Bible, we are told, "If it is possible, as far as it depends on you, live at peace with everyone." (Romans 12:18; NIV) I am a fan of this motto, and I wish that I could consistently live by it. This, however, is not always possible. Even if I didn't have to face the world, if I could avoid traffic, if my co-workers never disagreed...even then it would not be probable. Life involves other people, and relationships can get messy. Peace is a lofty goal, especially if we strive to live peacefully with everyone.

We have tried to make our home a peaceful place. When our children were young, Krista was a stay-at-home mom. I know that there were many days when she was dealing with some very non-peaceful situations. But she made it her goal to have the house feeling tranquil when I arrived home from work. Quiet music, a clean house, and rested children helped with this endeavor. Within minutes of my arrival, the peacefulness had disappeared, and it was often partly my fault. Picking up the kids, wrestling with them, and just enjoying being with my family ended the sound of peace. Ironically in those boisterous moments, there was still peace in our home and in our hearts.

Sometimes, during those early years of child-rearing, when the house was quiet at night and the kids were all asleep, the house seemed peaceful, but it wasn't. Balancing the family budget on one income, feeding and clothing four children, and the stressors of home maintenance would all surround me, and I found myself in a place of unrest. I concluded years ago that peace, true peace, is found in our hearts.

Krista and I have occasionally talked about selling our home and moving when our children have all moved out. We have several legitimate reasons for this, however none of our children are in support of this pursuit.

We moved into this house when our oldest child was less than two years old. None of our kids have memories of any other home. At times, I felt this house that we built in the middle of nowhere was too small. We often run into each other in the kitchen and our family Christmas get-togethers are crowded. However, my children LOVE this place. It is full of memories which walk hand in hand with the memories they will carry in their minds and in their hearts when they leave to go to their own homes someday. Amidst the fights, the disagreements, and the sharing of rooms, they remember the stories, the games, the campfires, and the picnics. They remember the love...the security...and they remember the peace!

I recall one Christmas Eve when a heavy snowstorm knocked out our power. We read the Christmas story from The Bible by candlelight. We opened our presents by kerosene lantern. We sang Christmas carols by firelight and the phrase "...sleep in Heavenly peace..." brought new meaning to our celebration.

Several friends from the city have often visited our home. As they sit on our deck sipping coffee in the morning or visit at our large kitchen table into the evening with the wind blowing the curtains, without exception they comment, "Your home is so peaceful." And without exception, I agree with them. I think a peaceful home comes with a contentment in life. It is accompanied by grateful hearts and sincere appreciation for others. This is a lesson we have tried to instill in each of our children. When we combine peace and gratitude, contentment and appreciation, we find ourselves facing life's demands with an optimistic view.

Landon once asked me, "Dad...how long can I live with you and Mom?" I smiled and assured him, "As long as you want, Buddy...as long as you want." Since then the topic still occasionally comes up. Realistically I know that the day may come when he does want to move out and be more on his own. We still have questions to answer, skills to learn, and battles to conquer, but for his sake, I hope that it happens someday, especially if it is a deep desire of his. For now, that's not our reality. For now, he will be here, in our peaceful home, with his mom and dad who are grateful for one that is not quite ready to leave the nest.

I don't talk about moving anymore. A few years ago, on a summer afternoon while sitting on my front porch, I came to that conclusion. The smell of the flowers, the song of the birds, the sound of the breeze through the wind chimes, the sight of the lake, and the memories within the walls of this home all got to me. I decided on that day that this is my home. This is my peace...and for now, Landon, Krista, and I are staying right here!

- Find peace and contentment within the walls of your home.

Raising a child with special needs has been a unique journey. My wife and I are now living with an adult with special needs, and it is a continuation of that trek. Through all the child-rearing years, we sought to treat Landon as we treated our other children. This included rules, discipline, and chores. Of course, at times, concessions and allowances had to be made due to seizure activity. I have been touched to watch his siblings not only show compassion and understanding, but also demonstrate their support and tenderness for him throughout these years. Sometimes, this has not been easy. Each of them has developed some amazing character traits in the process...traits of empathy and patience, those traits which will undoubtedly follow them into their adult lives and into their chosen professions.

Through all the rough times it was our goal to help Landon endure, thrive, and try to see the good amidst the challenges. In reality, his life has been a long lesson of teaching us those very things. He has shown us that blessings often follow suffering, and joy and sadness can co-exist. He has helped us look for the sunshine in the rain and search for the water in the desert. Through all his disappointments and setbacks, he has sustained hope. This has urged us to find and grasp that same hope. Our desire has been to help him find fulfillment in life. He has gone one step further. He has fully embraced life, and he is now enjoying employment where he is valued for who he is.

In all of this, we have also learned about our Heavenly Father. His love for us is beyond measure. He has walked this road with us. In the valleys, He has been there. On the mountaintops, He has been there. He has sustained us through the love of others. Landon's ongoing challenges do not diminish God's ability to heal in this world. Over time we have seen and accepted that Landon has influenced more people in this life through his disability than most people without a developmental challenge.

Landon has also accepted this. He recognizes God's plan for his life and His ultimate victory over seizures as he looks forward to eternity in Heaven, where they will not exist. It has been a journey that has brought us all to a clearer understanding of God, His faithfulness, and His ultimate plan for our good...and THAT is the greatest lesson of all!

I have wanted to write a book for many years. I started my first novel over 15 years ago but raising children and caring for a son with a seizure disorder took priority over writing. During those years I have started many books. They, too, sit unfinished. As I sat down last summer to write this book, which I had started in my head so many times before, I realized that my book about Landon had to be the first one that I published. It is the one that matters the most because of the journey on which it took us and all that we learned in the process.

As I near the completion of this project, I do so with a heart full of gratitude and peace. Through the telling of each of these stories, I have been reminded of the support and love we have felt through all the seasons of life. I have realized through this process how very fortunate my family and I have been. I pray that these narratives have touched you, as well. May our stories and our lessons bring you to a place in life where you find peace, joy, and contentment...wherever your journey is taking you.

- ONE FINAL THOUGHT...John 9:3b "...Jesus said, "But this happened so that the works of God might be displayed in him."

Made in the USA
Columbia, SC
02 June 2019